WRITING
AND
INSCRIPTION
IN
GOLDEN AGE
DRAMA

Purdue Studies in Romance Literatures

WRITING
AND
INSCRIPTION
IN
GOLDEN AGE
DRAMA

Charles Oriel

Purdue University Press
West Lafayette, Indiana

Library of Congress Cataloging-in-Publication Data
Oriel, Charles, 1954–
     Writing and inscription in Golden Age Drama / Charles Oriel.
        p. cm.   — (Purdue studies in Romance literatures)
     Originally presented as the author's thesis (George Washington
University, 1989).
     Includes bibliographical references and index.
     ISBN 1–55753–019–X (alk. paper)
     1. Spanish drama—Classical period, 1500–1700—History and
criticism. 2. Writing in literature. 3. Literature and society—Spain.
I. Title. II. Series.
PQ6105.O7 1992
862'.309—dc20 92-26368
                                                     CIP

Book and jacket design by Anita Noble

Printed in the United States of America

A Bertica

Contents

ix Acknowledgments

1 Introduction

21 Chapter One
Cultural Inscriptions: The Written and the Spoken
in Lope's *El villano en su rincón*

41 Chapter Two
Presence and Absence in *La estrella de Sevilla*

65 Chapter Three
"Seeing and Not Seeing": Interpretation and Drift in
Mira de Amescua's *El ejemplo mayor de la desdicha*

91 Chapter Four
Dangerous Scripts in Tirso's *Cautela contra cautela*

115 Chapter Five
Calderón's *La cisma de Inglaterra* and the Ethics
of Erasure

161 Supplement

167 Notes

173 Bibliography

185 Index

Acknowledgments

This project grew out of my doctoral dissertation, which I completed in 1989 at George Washington University. My first expression of thanks goes, therefore, to Inés Azar, who served as my dissertation director and who heroically put up with my many idiosyncrasies throughout the entire process. I thank her for her many *consejos magnánimos* and for the example that she continually set, both in and out of class.

I offer my heart-felt gratitude to the following individuals who have aided and abetted (whether consciously or not) in the process that has culminated in this book. Without their help, advice, and encouragement, it is very likely that this project would never have seen the light of day: Berta Bermúdez, Melodie Chu, Linda R. Cohn, Frederick A. de Armas, Steven Estroff, Susan L. Fischer, Thomas Fox, Charles Ganelin, David Grabel, Daniel L. Heiple, Catherine Larson, James A. Parr, Elias L. Rivers, Scott Rosenthal, Terri Sedran, and Bruce W. Wardropper.

I wish to thank my colleagues in the Department of Romance Languages and Literatures, Washington University, for their support: Nina Davis, John Garganigo, Mané Lagos, Alessandra Luiselli, Michael Mudrovic, Randolph Pope, Joseph Schraibman, and Elżbieta Skłodowska.

I owe a great debt to many at George Washington University, from whom I learned so much: Shirley Barnett, Erika Berry, Jim Burks, Judith Butler, Yvonne Captain-Hidalgo, Peter Caws, Michèle de Cruz-Sáenz, Elena Echeverría, Laura Franklin, Jack Frey, the late Guido Mazzeo, Tony Palmiero, José Quiroga, James Robb, Pilar Sáenz, Jean-Francois Thibault, and John Ziolkowski.

I thank the Department of Romance Languages and Literatures of Washington University for covering publication costs.

I am grateful to the Division of Sponsored Programs, Purdue Research Foundation, Purdue University, for their permission to reprint my earlier essay, "Deceptive Perceptions: The Metaphysics of Tirso's *Cautela contra cautela*," which appeared in *Romance Languages Annual* 2 (1991): 510-14, and which has been incorporated into Chapter Four of this book.

Finally, I thank my family for their faith, their love, and their support.

Introduction

¡Oh, malditos papeles, cuántos daños
habéis hecho en el mundo, que no hay suma
que los pueda contar; fuego os consuma,
que así dais ocasión de hacer engaños!
　　¡Cuántos en reinos propios y en extraños
levantasteis del suelo como espuma;
pero a veces volar con una pluma
suele venir a malograr los años!
　　¡Cuántos, sin culpa alguna, habréis culpado
por no poder saberse la disculpa!
¡Grande poder es un papel escrito!
　　Que sois testigos mudos del pecado;
y, siendo los terceros de la culpa,
venís a ser la prueba del delito.

$$(133b\text{-}34a)^1$$

There is no better or more appropriate introduction to the following essays than this sonnet from Lope de Vega's early drama *El galán escarmentado* (1598?). The speaker of these lines is Julio, a wealthy *converso* who has chanced upon some old love letters among his wife Ricarda's possessions. He immediately accuses her of dishonoring their marriage and, disregarding her protestations of innocence, angrily dismisses her. Julio utters a soliloquy—the sonnet quoted above—in which he specifically designates "papeles," the written word, as the explicit cause of an infinite number of "daños" and "engaños."

In an article on this little-studied *comedia*, the late Joseph H. Silverman has suggested that Julio's personal experience as a *converso* may well be behind the apparent bitterness he feels about the false proofs that are provided by written documents: "la violencia con que habla, la intensidad emocional con que describe el poder de un papel, nos indica que acaso esté

1

pensando a la vez en experiencias propias de otra índole o que había presenciado en la vida de otros individuos como él" (256).[2]

The written word in this sonnet constitutes a potentially powerful threat to personal honor in regard to two of its most important aspects, the sanctity of marriage and racial purity. Yet the nature of writing is apparently paradoxical in several ways: *papeles* may be used to establish and authenticate the truth of a given state of affairs, but they may also be exploited for the purpose of deception; although they are the "witnesses" of sin, they are "mute"; and though they are intimately involved in the machinations of "culpa," they are merely its "terceros." While purporting to be a proof, a bearer of truth, and thereby an authoritative preserver of the social order, written documents may also serve to subvert that order by virtue of that same authority.

This sonnet's questioning of the ambivalent status of the written (and printed) word is actually quite typical of the literature of this period, for it was precisely during Spain's Golden Age that many of the social, psychological, and epistemological implications of the graphic transmission of culture and knowledge started to become apparent. One of my basic contentions throughout this study is that Julio's impassioned diatribe against the written word is emblematic of a general problematizing of writing and inscription that may be found in much literature of the Spanish Golden Age.

The acts of reading and writing and their relation to representation (in general) and literature (in particular) have, of course, received increasing attention over the last several years from authors and critics alike. We have seen a proliferation of self-referential gestures in much recent fiction: an emphasizing of the processes and implications of reading and writing, such as that found in the work of Jorge Luis Borges or Italo Calvino, to name only two of many authors who come to mind. Borges's story "Pierre Menard, autor del *Quijote*," for example, concerns an author whose aim is to write a new version of Cervantes's classic that will coincide word for word with the original. Calvino's *If on a Winter's Night a Traveler* draws a complex web of relations between the possible authors, publishers, and readers (all represented within the world of Calvino's text) of a novel that goes by many names, one of which is *If on a Winter's Night a Traveler.* In this self-reflexive aspect, at least, such writers as Borges and Calvino are direct literary descendants of Cervantes and Laurence Sterne. This is a literature that concerns itself with its own processes of production and reception by self-consciously exposing and representing the implicit conventions by which all literary transactions occur.[3]

The problems connected with the acts of reading and writing have also received a great deal of attention recently from a growing number of theorists. In such works as *Interfaces of the Word* (1970) and *Orality and Literacy* (1982), Walter J. Ong, for example, has brilliantly examined written communication in terms of its differences from oral communication and has discussed the implications of those differences for Western culture as a whole. Oral communication, he tells us, necessarily takes place within a context of presence: in order to have it, a speaker and a listener must be mutually present.[4] On the other hand, written communication functions by way of absence, for a writer is normally absent, not only from the text, once it has been written, but from the reader as well. On both ends of a written communication—in both reading and writing—absence is fundamental and even appears to represent a figurative form of death:

> However unobtrusively, death presides at both ends of a writing operation. The basic reason is that the person being addressed as present is in fact absent and because, obversely, the author is not present to the reader although his words will be. The writer of the letter may even be dead by the time his words arrive at the locale to which they are sent. Or the reader presumed to be at the receiving end of the scribal operation may already be dead and buried when the letter is being penned to him by an unaware correspondent. (*Interfaces* 239)[5]

One early association of the written word with death is found in the New Testament, in 2 Corinthians 3.6, where the apostle Paul makes a clear distinction in an oft-quoted line between the *letter* and the *spirit*: ". . . the written code kills, but the Spirit gives life." Aside from its current usage, the term *spirit* is etymologically related to the notion of breath and breathing (from Latin *spiritus),* and it is but a short step from there to the notion of orality: the spoken word and the living, breathing person who has produced it. A clear dichotomy has been posited and a hierarchy established, one that appears to give positive value to spoken communication by making it both the image and carrier of truth, life, and spirit. By the same token, written communication "kills" or is, in and of itself, "dead."

Many of Ong's arguments, at least in this context, are something of a modern extension of this implied valorization. In various works he examines in great detail the distinctions between the two types of communication. Absence and presence, he reminds us, are established on the fundamental levels of space and time, and the spoken word, as part of the oral/aural universe, exists only within the continuum of time—within, that is, the present moment: "Sound exists only when it is going out of existence: in uttering the word *existence*, by the time I get to the *-tence*, the *exis-* is gone and has to be gone. . . . The real word, the spoken word, is always an event . . . an action, an ongoing part of ongoing existence" (*Interfaces* 20-21).[6] Writing, on the other hand, remains outside the flow of time and outside of the present moment, for it is oriented toward both the past and the future. It is oriented toward the past in that it is utilized to fix and record history; the written word can do this by virtue of:

> a special involvement with the past, namely its textuality as such. Not just what a text says, but the physical text itself possesses a certain pastness. Unlike an utterance, a text is assimilated by the person who receives it not when it is being composed but after its utterance . . . is over with. . . . A text is simply there, something over with, a thing out of the past. (232)

By the same token, the written word is oriented toward the future because it reaches posterity by outlasting speech. But not, declares Ong, without certain drawbacks:

> The kind of life writing enjoys remains bizarre, for it is achieved at the price of death. The words that "live" are inert, as no real words can ever be. They are no longer audible, which is to say they are no longer real words, but only marks on the surface which can signal those who know the proper codes. (234)

The act of speaking, relative to that of writing, might be called "existential": it is in the "here and now," while the act of writing is always "there and then," literally removed and absent.

By virtue of its dependence upon presence, the spoken word is born of a particular and determined communicative context. Context, in fact, radically determines the nature and content of the oral communication. This dependence upon immediate context is similar to that which Barbara Herrnstein Smith has established as one of the essential aspects of what she calls "natural discourse," which consists of "the verbal acts of real persons on particular occasions in response to particular sets of circumstances" (15). As a "natural utterance," the spoken word is always an *event*, whose meaning is born of the specific context in which it was produced.

The written word, however, is liberated from any such immediate context by virtue of its textuality. It is outside of the "here and now," for the distinct moments of its production and its reception are separated by potentially vast amounts of space and time. Relative to oral communication, it offers little firm ground on which to stand. It is an object unto itself which appears to create its own context and reality and which more often than not is subject to those contexts and realities that the reader wishes independently to impose upon it.

It is precisely this independence of the written text and its implications for the literary process that has attracted the attention of such contemporary theorists as Roland Barthes and Jacques Derrida. Barthes makes reference to what Jonathan Culler since has called the inherent "monumentality" of all written texts (*Structuralist* 133-34). It is this monumentality that, in part, distinguishes written from spoken communication:

> All modes of writing have in common the fact of being "closed" and thus different from spoken language. Writing is in no way an instrument for communication, it is not an open route through which there passes only the intention to speak . . . writing is a hardened language which is self-contained. . . . What makes writing the opposite of speech is that the former always *appears* symbolical, introverted, ostensibly turned toward an occult side of language, whereas the second is nothing but a flow of empty signs, the movement of which alone is significant. . . . Writing . . . is always

> rooted in something beyond language . . . it manifests an
> essence and holds the threat of a secret, it is an anticom-
> munication, it is intimidating. (Barthes, *Writing* 19-20)

Barthes emphasizes the opposition between speech's sense of
process—its openness and mobility—and the written word's
closure, fixity, and secrecy. Relative to oral communication,
written communication is always "other," always deferred.

Jacques Derrida has often pointed out that writing's apparent ambiguity and secrecy have inspired its general denuncia-
tion throughout much of the Western philosophical tradition as
"secondary," "artificial," and "exterior," relative to oral communication (*Grammatology* 34-35). Until fairly recently, for
example, the accepted notion of the process of reading went
something like this: confronted by an ambiguous or multi-
leveled piece of writing, a reader would attempt to give it unity
by imposing upon it an essential meaning, an "ultimate" intention. The reader would attempt to re-create the original context
of presence and *voice* that stands behind and produces the writing. By imposing the criteria of orality upon that which was
written, a phenomenon that functions by way of absence was
forced to conform to the mode of presence. It is only relatively
recently, with the advent of structuralism and poststructuralism,
that this model has begun to be seriously challenged. The
deconstructionists and Derrida in particular have pointed out
this "metaphysics of presence" that has systematically pre-
ferred oral to written communication, a metaphysics that has,
according to Derrida, dominated much of Western thought:

> For a writing to be a writing, it must continue to "act" and to
> be readable even when what is called the author of the writ-
> ing no longer answers for what he has written, for what he
> seems to have signed, be it because of a temporary absence,
> because he is dead or, more generally, because he has not
> employed his absolutely actual and present intention or at-
> tention, the plenitude of his desire to say what he means, in
> order to sustain what seems to be written "in his name." . . .
> This essential drift [*dérive*] bearing on writing as an itera-
> tive structure, cut off from all absolute responsibility, from
> *consciousness* as the ultimate authority, orphaned and sepa-
> rated at birth from the assistance of its father, is precisely
> what Plato condemns in the *Phaedrus*. ("Signature" 8)

The written word's status as an "orphan" and its "iterative structure, cut off from all absolute responsibility," make it subject to a potentially infinite "drift" and interpretability.[7] This is what makes it most objectionable to that traditional metaphysical longing for absolute presence and truth, a longing of which much of Ong's work is clearly a more modern manifestation.

Derrida utilizes various terms to describe the metaphysical tradition's "logocentrism," that is, its valorization of the (spoken) *logos* in terms of presence and as the origin and bearer of absolute truth, as well as its obvious corollary: a consistent bias against the written word. Writing, he tells us, has consistently been accused of "supplementarity" in relation to spoken communication. Derrida notes as an example Rousseau's thinking in "Essay on the Origin of Languages":

> . . . speech being natural or at least the natural expression of thought, . . . writing is added to it, is adjoined, as an image or representation. In that sense, it is not natural. It diverts the immediate presence of thought to speech into representation and the imagination. This recourse is not only "bizarre," but dangerous. It is the addition of a technique, a sort of artificial and artful ruse to make speech present when it is actually absent. It is a violence done to the natural destiny of language. (*Grammatology* 144)

According to this tradition, writing is an artificial and exterior addition to oral speech that inevitably distorts and perverts the ostensible purity of the "original": "writing, the letter, the sensible inscription, has always been considered by Western tradition as the body and matter external to the spirit, to breath, to speech, and to the logos" (35). It is Derrida's claim, of course, that there is no such original, full, and absolute presence and that such supplementarity is, in fact, one of the constitutive factors of all forms of communication, of all "texts." He suggests, in short, that speaking *is* a type of writing: "writing is at the same time more exterior to speech, not being its 'image' or its 'symbol,' and more interior to speech, which is already in itself a writing" (46). Derrida extends this notion to other areas:

> . . . we say "writing" for all that gives rise to an inscription in general, whether it is literal or not and even if what it distributes in space is alien to the order of the voice:

> cinematography, choreography, of course, but also picto-
> rial, musical, sculptural "writing." One might also speak of
> athletic writing and with even greater certainty of military
> or political writing in view of the techniques that govern
> those domains today. All this is to describe not only the sys-
> tem of notation secondarily connected with these activities
> but the essence and the content of the activities themselves. (9)

Derrida's use of the term *inscription* is, of course, broadly figurative. It denotes the prescribed codes, whether literally written out or not, that govern all cultural activity. It makes explicit
that there is a form of inscription or textuality behind all forms
of cognizance, that there is literally "nothing outside the text."
The implication is that such value-laden terms as *truth* and
reality are neither given nor natural to any particular situation,
but are inevitably mediated by historically and culturally
determined conventions. According to this way of thinking,
"reality" is always a construct.

In "Plato's Pharmacy," Derrida analyzes Plato's *Phaedrus*,
which he identifies as one of the starting points of the metaphysical tradition's bias against writing. In Plato's dialogue,
Socrates describes how the Egyptian king Thamus criticized
the god Theuth's new invention—writing—by calling it a
pharmakon, meaning both "cure" and "poison": "Those who
acquire it will cease to exercise their memory and become for-
getful; they will rely on writing to bring things to their remem-
brance by external signs instead of on their own internal
resources. What you have discovered is a *receipt* for recollec-
tion, not for memory" (96). Socrates himself then proceeds to
attack the written word on his own terms:

> it shows great folly . . . to suppose that one can transmit or
> acquire clear and certain knowledge of an art through the
> medium of writing, or that written words can do more than
> remind the reader of what he already knows on any given
> subject. . . . writing involves a similar disadvantage to paint-
> ing. The productions of painting look like human beings, but
> if you ask them a question they maintain a solemn silence.
> The same holds true of written words; you might suppose
> that they understand what they are saying, but if you ask
> them what they mean by anything they simply return the
> same answer over and over again. Besides, once a thing is
> committed to writing it circulates equally among those who

> understand the subject and those who have no business with
> it; a writing cannot distinguish between suitable and unsuit-
> able readers. And if it is ill-treated or unfairly abused it
> always needs its parent to come to its rescue; it is quite
> incapable of defending or helping itself. (97)

According to Plato's Socrates, the written word is an artificial
addition, a *supplement*, that may serve to remedy the weakness
of memory but at the same time poisons it by creating a depen-
dency upon itself (Culler, *Deconstruction* 142).

I have very briefly touched upon some of Derrida's concepts
here because they will be found in different contexts throughout this study. His view of writing and orality and of the relation between them provides a crucial counterpoint to that of
Ong. I do not pretend to reconcile such radically opposed systems of thought, nor do I wish to imply that they could be
reconciled, for whereas much of Ong's work constitutes a
"metaphysics of presence" that subordinates writing to orality,
much of Derrida's constitutes a relentless critique of that metaphysics. For this reason, Derrida's use of certain concepts, such
as *supplementarity, drift, pharmakon, différance,* and *erasure,*
is particularly useful in identifying and describing the functionality of writing and inscription in these dramas, a functionality
that is often governed by that same metaphysics of presence.
These essays are, in effect, an examination of that metaphysics
in the *comedia.*

There are, however, many points of intersection and general
agreement between Ong and Derrida. Indeed, Ong's pioneer-
ing early examinations of the cultural implications of writing
and inscription could be seen as implicitly providing the basis
for later developments, including many of the observations
offered by Derrida. The result is that the work of both Ong and
Derrida helps to provide a theoretical context, a type of dialogue in which the opposition of written and oral communication may be profitably considered. Both theorists, for example,
base their discussions of this opposition upon the broader one
of presence/absence, even though their conceptions and their
uses of these terms may radically differ. This last opposition—
presence/absence—is the true focus of this study.

The crisis of sensibility inspired by that opposition and
others that are related to it—truth/fiction, nature/culture,

interiority/exteriority, spirit/body, self/other, private/public—
is perhaps what best characterizes the particular tensions of the
age in which the *comedia* came into being. The dialogical
opposition between Ong and Derrida therefore provides a fitting analogue to the whole complex of social, political, psychological, spiritual, and epistemological concerns which in large
part define the period that we now refer to as the Golden Age.

Historically speaking, of course, the wide circulation of written and printed material—books—was a relatively new phenomenon in the sixteenth century. Until that time, in fact, all
books had been handwritten by scribes and were found almost
exclusively in churches, monasteries, palaces, or universities.
The vast majority of the people of Western Europe—that is, the
"popular" mentality—was still largely oriented toward and
dominated by the oral transmission of history, knowledge, and
culture. And, as far as books went, there was, throughout the
Middle Ages and up until the end of the fifteenth century, really
only one book that had made a truly lasting impression upon
the popular sensibility. This one book, however, had become,
through a very long process, the centerpiece of Western culture:
the Bible.

It is with the invention of the printing press, around the
middle of the fifteenth century, that this situation began to
change. With the possibility of mass production afforded by
movable type, the wider circulation of books throughout the
general populace had started to become a reality. The Bible
ceased to be the *only* book; there was now a variety of books,
some of them appearing to differ from and even oppose the
original Word, at least as it was defined and propagated by that
central authority, the Roman Catholic Church.

In a stimulating study of the reading habits of this period,
B. W. Ife stresses the new sense of individualism that was pro-
moted by the private act of reading:

> Having welcomed the press at first, the clergy soon found
> that by encouraging the reading of devotional literature they
> had made a rod for their own backs. Once set loose the
> demon book could not be kept under control. The public
> could not be prevented from reading what it liked or from
> imposing its own tastes on publishers and writers. Works of
> devotion were pushed from pride of place and imaginative

literature began to impinge on areas of emotion which the Church wanted reserved for religious feeling. In Spain, opposition to literature seems to form part of a general Catholic opposition to the ideals of *pietas litterata*, to the promotion of scripture in the vernacular, and the consequent elimination of the clergy's role as exegetes of the Word and intermediaries between man and God. The unacceptable directness and the individualist nature of literary experience inevitably smacked of a Protestant frame of mind, and Spanish clergymen countered with their traditional mistrust of the layman's ability to cope unaided with dangerous things like thoughts and feelings. (12)

The printing press also had (and continues to have) radical implications for the popular notion of textuality. Prior to the invention of movable type, books inevitably retained human traces, that is, the handwriting of the person who had transcribed them. Ernst Robert Curtius has noted in *European Literature and the Latin Middle Ages* the importance of this fundamental change:

> . . . to reading conceived as the form of reception and study, corresponds writing conceived as the form of production and creation. The two concepts belong together. In the intellectual world of the Middle Ages they represent as it were the two halves of a sphere. The unity of this world was shattered by the invention of printing. The immense and revolutionary change which it brought about can be summarized in one statement: Until that time, every book was a manuscript. Merely materially, then, as well as artistically, the written book had a value which we can no longer feel. Every book produced by copying represented diligence and skilled craftsmanship, long hours of intellectual concentration, loving and sedulous work. Every such book was a personal achievement . . . (328)

The act of reading had always been necessarily preceded by an act of handwriting; one could not read *except* that which had been inscribed by a living, breathing person. It is interesting to see how Curtius frames his discussion of reading and writing in terms of an "ideal" unity. He emphasizes the personal, human element that was an inherent part of every book: there is, in effect, something of a "metaphysics of presence" behind

Introduction

Curtius's words, one that is, historically speaking, absolutely justified. Despite the fact that the written text represented a form of deferral and absence (of the creator/producer of the text and its reader), that hiatus had always been mediated by a scribe, whose traces could be felt and whose human presence was thereby easily projected or imagined by the reader. But the technology of printing defers even more radically this sense of human presence: the original act of creation/production is even further absented.

With the wider circulation of printed materials, therefore, and with this more radical sense of *absence* that is one of its results, comes the start of the privatization of culture, both spiritual and secular. This privatization came about, in large part, because the transmission of knowledge and ideas was no longer public and communal, no longer exclusively orally-based. It had become largely a private, silent—and thereby secret and possibly subversive—process: reading and writing.

The appearance of written or inscribed texts in many Spanish Golden Age *comedias* is a matter that has received very little specific critical attention. This is rather surprising, given the frequency with which written texts do appear and the extent to which they make themselves felt as pivotal elements in individual dramas. A good starting point is T. Earle Hamilton's 1947 essay, "Spoken Letters in the *Comedias* of Alarcón, Tirso and Lope." This article represents the first explicit and sustained critical attention (of which I am aware) given to this motif in the *comedia*. Perhaps the best summary of this article is Hamilton's own clear and concise statement of purpose, which is:

> to compare the form of the letter in the *comedias* of Lope, Tirso, and Alarcón. To establish the manner in which Alarcón differs from Lope and Tirso, my inquiry is extended to several subsidiary or related topics, as follows: (1) the distribution of letters, (2) the distribution of verse forms in letters, (3) the distribution of verse forms which precede and follow letters, (4) the percentage of letters read completely, (5) the percentage of letters with interruptions, (6) the presence of broken strophes or verses, (7) letters used to begin or end a scene, (8) cryptic letters with two or more meanings, and (9) the choice of prose or verse by different classes of characters. (63)

Hamilton's essay is important because it marks out new ground for critical investigation. Despite its general and rather schematic nature, the essay contains some interesting information, but is obviously limited by the decision to consider only *letters* that are read aloud in various dramas, without any mention of other forms of inscription that either appear explicitly or merely by way of reference within the dialogue itself. Hamilton's study is essentially a statistical survey which, interesting though it might be, offers little in the way of sustained consideration as to the aesthetic function or significance of such letters. (In all fairness, the author himself recognizes that this latter aspect is simply not his focus in this particular piece, claiming in a footnote [63] that he has "left the function of the letter for later consideration." I do not know of any follow-up article to this one.)

Another essay on the subject of inscribed documents in the *comedia* is Henri Recoules's "Cartas y papeles en el teatro del siglo de oro" (1974). Aside from proposing several questions that seem basic to any investigation of this topic, this article is essentially a listing, drama by drama, of explicit appearances of letters and papers in most of the works of Lope, Tirso, and Calderón. Recoules's ambitious list has certain drawbacks, however. It includes, for example, only those *comedias* of Lope found in the thirteen-volume *Obras* (1916) published by the Real Academia Española. This edition was intended to give wider circulation to many of Lope's lesser-known dramas and as a result contains very few of his better-known ones. Recoules also limits himself to explicit appearances of written texts onstage and, like Hamilton, does not include any consideration of spoken references that characters might make to writing, either literal or figurative. Despite these drawbacks, his article contains a wealth of useful and specific information: which dramas contain explicit appearances of written texts, where they appear within the text, their physical form (letters, books, inscriptions) and their literary form (prose or verse). The greatest merit of Recoules's essay lies, finally, in the simple fact that, like Hamilton's, it draws attention to an area that has received almost no critical attention at all.

Elias L. Rivers has made some extremely important contributions to the study of the "dialectical" opposition of writing and orality. Besides his *Quixotic Scriptures* (1983), which masterfully traces the interplay of these two traditions throughout

e entire trajectory of Spanish literature, Rivers has also writ-
:n two articles that insightfully examine this opposition in the
specific context of Golden Age drama: "The Shame of Writing
in *La Estrella de Sevilla*" (1980) and "Written Poetry and Oral
Speech Acts in Calderón's Plays" (1983). More recently, Paul
Julian Smith has brilliantly investigated cultural inscription
and the various manifestations of supplementarity or excess
in Spanish Golden Age literature in *Writing in the Margin:
Spanish Literature of the Golden Age* (1988), a suggestive and
influential study that borrows heavily from deconstructive
thought. Aside from these basic works, Frederick A. de Armas
examines "poison letters" and their relation to the *pharmakon*
in "Baltasar's Doom: Letters that Heal/Kill in Claramonte's *El
secreto en la mujer*" (forthcoming). Finally, in a new and illu-
minating study, *Language and the Comedia* (1991), Catherine
Larson provocatively explores the interplay between writing
and orality that takes place in Lope's *Fuenteovejuna*.

Inscribed texts appear in many guises in Golden Age dramas.
They may appear explicitly onstage in the form of letters, notes,
books, decrees, petitions, and even as inscriptions on coins, on
stones, or in bronze, or they may be merely referred to or mentioned by a particular character. Writing is often invoked figuratively, as when a character refers to the constellations as the
"hieroglyphics" of Fate or when someone's fame is spoken of
as being eternal and therefore impervious to "erasure" by the
passage of time. As a literary genre, drama is particularly
effective in its foregrounding of written texts because, unlike
other written and printed literary genres, it has a performative
dimension that is essentially oral. As a result, written texts that
appear in drama have an inherent irony that draws attention to
them as objects worthy of question: we are forced by the very
nature of dramatic art to sit up and take notice.

Although a theatrical presentation or performance combines
visual and oral aspects, it is clear that the most common mode
of reception of Spanish Golden Age drama in our own time is
textual, that is, via the private act of reading. In *The Semiotics
of Theatre and Drama* (1980), Keir Elam thus distinguishes the
theatrical or "performance" text from the written or "dramatic"
text (2-3). All drama is, in reality, a "hybrid" that derives from
and combines elements of the written and oral traditions. Rivers
makes this clear in his essay on Calderón:

> In the classical literary tradition of the Western World, drama
> is unique in preserving so many pre-literate (or oral) ele-
> ments as contemporaneous with literate (or written) modes
> of conceiving the text as fixed upon a piece of paper. The
> Spanish language makes us aware of the hybrid nature of
> dramatic literature when it speaks of actors performing a
> "paper" or role, "los actores que desempeñan su papel, el
> papel escrito por el poeta, el papel que define en términos
> de actos verbales al carácter del personaje evocado por el
> actor." ("Written" 271)

Any dramatic performance—its plot, its situations, its characters—is literally pre-scribed and pre-determined by a written
text that has been produced by a playwright. The roles played
by individual actors onstage are also *papeles* in the most literal
sense: pieces of paper that prescribe the verbal and physical acts
that they are to perform. In this sense, drama as a literary genre
literalizes Derrida's notion that there is a form of inscription
behind even the most seemingly spontaneous activities and that
speaking *is,* in fact, "a type of writing." Indeed, the very term
perform (per-form) implies a pre-established model or "form"—
a pre-text—according to which certain actions are to be carried
out. As such, drama constitutes an "intersection," a place where
orality and writing necessarily co-exist.

In his chapter on the *comedia* in *Writing in the Margin*, Paul
Julian Smith argues in much the same direction:

> Drama continues to call into question the integrity of the sub-
> ject and the prestige of representation because the performer
> is at once equal to and greater than the presence of the body
> on stage. The actor, unlike the author, is present to the
> audience and material to their perception. But that presence
> is determined by a supplementary or surplus value which is
> itself immaterial: the actor's status as "character" or fictional
> agent. Drama thus reproduces in the very conditions of its
> possibility the necessary excess common to writing as a
> whole. (128)

Smith's point is, of course, very similar to Rivers's, except that
his argument is clothed in the terminology that we now asso-
ciate with deconstruction.

By so consciously utilizing and underlining the opposition
between written and oral communication, much Golden Age

drama appears to make manifest certain social, philosophical, and cultural trends. The new status, authority, and widespread diffusion of written texts and books was starting to be seriously questioned in various ways by culture as a whole. This transition can be seen in changes in the very concept of textuality and, by extension, of literature itself, as Rivers has noted: "By converting evanescent spoken words and phrases into fixed inscriptions, writing introduced the concept of the text as separable from both writer and reader . . ." ("Written" 273).

One Golden Age document that dramatizes this sometimes painful transition is *Don Quijote*, a text that compulsively puts itself to questioning—explicitly and implicitly—the status and authority of nearly every genre of written discourse that had been produced by Western culture up until that point, including its own. As Robert Alter has so concisely stated, "The novel begins out of an erosion of belief in the authority of the written word and it begins with Cervantes" (3). In short, the "anomaly" represented by the rapid diffusion of written and printed texts (a distinctly post-Gutenberg phenomenon) is paralleled by their "anomalous" appearance within the essentially oral world of dramatic performance. By highlighting inscribed texts in this way, these dramas appear to question their status and value as means of communication, as bearers of "truth," as functional institutions of society.

In questioning the status of written texts as institutions, these dramas question the status of other forms of cultural inscription as well: the monarchy, the code of honor, in short, nearly every institution that serves as a base and context for society itself. How this is done differs from drama to drama, although certain elements remain fairly constant. The act of writing, for example, always implies some sense of absence and, by extension, secrecy. Thus it is that written texts may serve as a vehicle for social subversion, depending upon who is doing the writing, who the reading, and in what particular context. However, when written texts appear in association with a king they tend to have a public function rather than a private one. In such contexts writing becomes a force of social order: a means of imposing, by decree, the law.[8]

This last function is essentially what is enacted in Lope de Vega's *El villano en su rincón* (1611), the drama studied in Chapter One. A wealthy farmer named Juan Labrador has written his own epitaph, a strange inscription that says that he never saw the King or suffered any misfortune. Despite the fact that the act of writing an epitaph conventionally assumes the prior death of the person to whom it refers, no date of death is given. When the King reads it, he recognizes that the epitaph constitutes a subversive challenge not only to natural and civic law (which he, as monarch, institutionally upholds) but also to the law of God. By the end of the drama, however, the King forces Juan to come to court, to see him, and to recognize his law and his reign. The King accomplishes this largely by way of letters and written decrees. What started out as the mutual absence of Juan Labrador and the King evolves by way of the play's action into mutual, permanent, and royally decreed presence when the monarch orders Juan to serve him as *mayordomo* for the rest of his life.

The opposing utilization of writing occurs in the anonymous *La estrella de Sevilla* (1623), studied in Chapter Two. In this drama, the King, the supposed fount and base of social order, is himself its subverter. This subversion is the result of a devious shuffling of public and private priorities: in effect, King Sancho uses his public office to procure the objects of his private desires. Such privatization is manifested metaphorically in the drama, for he attempts to accomplish his desires by way of that most private and secretive of means, written texts. Social subversion occurs in this play primarily by way of written notes and documents. It is only through orality and full *presence* that the King is finally forced to live up to and take full responsibility for his own acts.

The third chapter examines Antonio Mira de Amescua's *El ejemplo mayor de la desdicha* (1625). This drama belongs to a subgenre of the *comedia* known as *dramas de privanza*, which deal with the rise and fall of *privados* or court favorites. The protagonist, Belisario, is a victim of the turbulent and violent nature of court intrigue and pays with his life for the position of power he has reached. The drama is dominated by images of visual perception that serve to manifest the darkness, the essential ambiguity, of human experience. In the end, it is a written document, a letter, that helps to bring about his downfall. Throughout the drama, in fact, various *papeles* (in all the senses of the term) serve to emphasize the ultimate ambiguity of all perception and the arbitrary quality of Fate.

Chapter Four studies Tirso de Molina's *Cautela contra cautela* (1621?). Like Mira de Amescua's *El ejemplo,* it dramatizes the dangerous opposition between ostensible appearances and reality. Unlike *El ejemplo*, however, the action of Tirso's play is almost wholly generated by this opposition. The result is an intricate plot of courtly intrigue that is even further complicated by a consistent use of role-playing that functions so as to victimize even those who perpetrate it. This form of metatheater serves to emphasize the ambiguity and consequent danger of all exterior appearances and signs, such as the written word.

Chapter Five deals with Calderón's *La cisma de Inglaterra* (1627?). Set in England during the reign of Henry VIII, this play, like *La estrella de Sevilla,* dramatizes the tragic results of a monarchy that is led by passion to disregard its own publicly proclaimed standards of ethics. From the very first scene, various aspects of textuality—reading, re-reading, writing, rewriting, and erasure—play a large part, both functionally (in terms of the action) and metaphorically, in the trajectory of passion and death which is enacted. The concept of textuality takes on further meaning when we consider that Calderón's play itself constitutes a rewriting of English history within the context of the ideological opposition between Catholicism and Protestantism.

Each of these five dramas is by a different author, yet all demonstrate a consistent preoccupation with the status, use, and function of writing and inscription. In choosing dramas by different playwrights, I hope to show that the phenomenon under discussion in this study is not limited to any single author or school, but is, rather, a vital part of the general consciousness of the age.

The lack of any *comedia de capa y espada* among those studied will be conspicuous to some, if for no other reason than that there were more *comedias* of this type produced than any other. In excluding such dramas from my study, I have followed the lead of one of the great modern *comediantes*, Bruce W. Wardropper, who refers to seventeenth-century theorist Francisco Bances Candamo's[9] distinction between *comedias de capa y espada* and other more "serious" works:

> . . . las comedias de capa y espada se sitúan en el *hic et nunc*;
> se proponen reflejar, remedar, satirizar o caricaturizar las

maneras de la juventud de la hidalguía urbana. En este
aspecto contrastan con obras graves como *Fuenteovejuna*
(cuya acción transcurre en el siglo XV) y *La vida es sueño*
(situada en Polonia). Los hechos que hay que contemplar con
seriedad precisan de una distanciación temporal o espacial
respecto del espectador. ("La comedia" 195)

The dramas studied in the following essays may be considered
"obras graves" in precisely this sense of distance. Without
exception, they are distanced both spatially and temporally
from seventeenth-century Madrid. *El villano en su rincón* is set
in medieval France; the action of *La estrella de Sevilla* occurs
in thirteenth-century Seville; *El ejemplo mayor de la desdicha* is set in Justinian's reign over the Eastern Roman Empire
during the sixth century; the action of *Cautela contra cautela*
transpires in fifteenth-century Naples; and finally, *La cisma de
Inglaterra* is set in early sixteenth-century England. Unlike the
vast majority of *comedias de capa y espada*, each of these dramas represents an episode or theme that appears exotic by virtue of this temporal and spatial distancing. I have not meant to
deny the artistry, the beauty, or the importance of the *comedias
de capa y espada* by their exclusion from this study; it is simply that I have found myself drawn to those *comedias* that are
more eccentrically problematical or atypical. Indeed, one
would be hard-put even to use the word *comic* in connection
with any of these dramas, despite the all-encompassing use of
the term *comedia* throughout the seventeenth century. With the
possible exceptions of *El villano en su rincón* and *Cautela
contra cautela*—and even these two have certain elements of
tragedy—they tend toward what we now call the *tragic*. Three
of them—*El villano, La estrella,* and *La cisma*—are part of the
canon of widely read *comedias*. The other two—*El ejemplo* and
Cautela—are, relatively speaking, "marginal" texts that have
scarcely been examined.

The structuralist and poststructuralist modes of thought have
fostered a relentless questioning of many of the most basic
assumptions that govern literary practices, both "creative" and
"critical." It is in precisely such a context of self-reflection and
self-questioning that these Golden Age dramas, which represent the images of their own creation as written texts, provide
a fitting point of departure for a rigorous re-examination of

many of the basic institutional codes that underlie the worlds represented within those dramas and those that underlie our own. By focusing on the preoccupation with writing and inscription that these dramas demonstrate, we may better be able to describe how they help to document the transition to modernity.

Chapter One

Cultural Inscriptions

The Written and the Spoken in Lope's
El villano en su rincón

Despite the great amount of critical attention that Lope de Vega's *El villano en su rincón* (1611) has justly received, very little has focused on one of its most important elements: the function of writing and written texts. An examination of this aspect helps to make explicit the drama's structure, which is based upon such clear oppositions as village/court, speaking/writing, reading/writing, things/texts, and nature/culture.

Like so many Golden Age dramas, *El villano* has two lines of action, one of which is subordinated to the other. The secondary plot is a simple love intrigue involving Lisarda (the daughter of Juan Labrador, a wealthy *campesino*) and Otón, a courtier. They meet and fall in love when Lisarda, disguised as a lady of the court, visits Paris. Various obstacles to their love, including the disparity between them in social status, are overcome when Lisarda is sent to court by her father, as per the King's order, and becomes one of the Princess's ladies-in-waiting. This line of action reaches a happy resolution when the King orders their marriage in the final scene.

The primary plot involving Juan Labrador and the King of France is of most concern here, for the evolution and the implications of their relation are the main focus of this chapter. When the King reads Juan's strange epitaph, he is surprised to learn that one of his subjects would so studiously avoid him and decides to meet the person. Disguised as a courtier, he goes to visit Juan, who receives him with all due hospitality and, questioned by the visitor, swears complete loyalty to the King. Soon thereafter, the King writes a letter to Juan requesting a loan. Juan readily complies. The King then writes once again, this time requesting that Juan send his son and daughter to Paris. Juan again complies. The King then orders Juan himself to come to court. When he arrives, the King appoints him *mayor-domo*, in which capacity he is to serve at court for the rest of his life; so ends the drama.

El villano's action is divided between two locales, the country village that is Juan's home and the court in Paris. The opposition between these two places is emphasized throughout and is paralleled by the opposition between the two principal characters who are their best representatives, Juan Labrador and the King. At the beginning of the drama, Juan proudly defines himself—both in person and in his own prematurely written epitaph—as a confirmed villager who never saw either King or court. The drama's action is resolved in such a way that this self-definition is flatly contradicted, for not only will Juan see the King and the court before he dies, but in his new position as *mayordomo* he will unquestionably have a personal and intimate relationship with the King every day for the rest of his life. The two plots of *El villano* enact the various oppositions mentioned above, all of which will be examined in this chapter, but it is the opposition of written and spoken communication that is its specific focus.

The first written text that appears in *El villano en su rincón* is Juan's epitaph:

> "Yace aquí Juan Labrador,
> que nunca sirvió a señor,
> ni vio la corte, ni al Rey,
> ni temió ni dio temor;
> ni tuvo necesidad,
> ni estuvo herido ni preso,
> ni en muchos años de edad
> vio en su casa mal suceso,
> envidia ni enfermedad."
>
> (735-43)

These written words have a specific and defined permanence that is all the more emphasized by their being inscribed in stone. They represent the past with apparent officiality yet continue to exist on into the future as well. This seemingly limitless life of the written word is implied by the epitaph, which, significantly, does not contain the date of Juan's death. It is as though an implicit analogy has been posited between Juan Labrador and his own words: the ostensible permanence of the inscribed epitaph is paralleled by Juan's seemingly limitless (i.e., no date of death) life.

The omission of the date of death, however, makes the inscription into something of a self-contradiction because it means that Juan is still alive. He does not, in fact, "lie here," as the epitaph states. The logical presupposition of any epitaph is, of course, the prior death of the person to whom it refers. It is impossible for Juan or anyone else to write an epitaph that truly recounts his or her own (complete) life, because as long as one is alive the possibility remains that one's life and, consequently, one's final epitaph might change. John E. Varey emphasizes this point in his article on *El villano*: "Since the epitaph is necessarily written before the writer's life is ended, it is clear that this statement, in the normal course of human affairs, may be subject to change . . ." (318).[1]

In Part 1 of *Don Quijote*, of course, Cervantes has given us what is perhaps the best-known and most explicit presentation of the inherent limits of all autobiographical discourse, of which Juan's epitaph is an example. When Ginés de Pasamonte, a seeming incarnation of the picaresque genre, reveals that he has written the story of his own life and Don Quijote asks him if it is finished, the former responds ironically with a question of his own: "¿Cómo puede estar acabado . . . si aún no está acabada mi vida?" (1.272). One of the conventions by which epitaphs are granted authority is the assumption that they are written by someone who has survived the persons to whom they refer. Under normal circumstances, an individual's epitaph is the responsibility of those for whom, by way of death, that person has become "history."

In this context, death represents the ultimate absence, and history, as a specifically inscribed institution, is inherently dependent upon absence, for its conventional function is to represent that which was but no longer is. Juan attempts to establish himself as institutional authority by utilizing the standard mode of historical narration—the past tense—to refer to events that are still evolving in the present, namely, his own life. In so doing, he challenges the basis of history as institution, for he claims by way of the epitaph to be historical. The fact that he is still alive and well makes that claim false. In short, Juan's writing of his own epitaph implies a logical contradiction: the identity of temporal presence and temporal absence. This is neatly symbolized in the epitaph itself, a text that has been inscribed on an explicitly physical and solid *thing*: "absence" is, figuratively speaking, inscribed upon "presence." The inscription thus appears to be a strange and unsettling mixture of the two, for its referential value is contradicted by the very reality to which it refers and, given this context, becomes an anomalous and ambivalent cross between a prediction and an order.

In the language of speech act theory, the circumstances surrounding Juan's epitaph subvert the illocutionary force that is conventionally associated with epitaphs. Under normal circumstances—i.e., the prior death of the person to whom it refers—epitaphs are *assertives*, that is, statements that refer to and describe an event or a state of things in the world. This epitaph has, rather, the illocutionary force of a *prediction*, for it refers to an event that is still in the process of occurring: Juan's *complete* life.[2]

Words that are inscribed on stone have a monumentality that gives them a public and official sense. They have the authority of a general announcement that is seemingly *from* nobody in particular *to* nobody in particular. In the case of Juan's epitaph, this authority seems even greater, for it states his independence in such an absolute way ("que nunca sirvió a señor, / ni vio la corte, ni al Rey, / ni temió ni dio temor") that it appears to aspire to the force of an almost royal imperative. The inscription seems to speak with absolute authority and to demand a controlled and passive response on the part of its readers, including the King himself. In this sense, Juan usurps the institutional role of the monarch and implicitly challenges the order and authority that he represents.

The King, for his part, can do nothing other than interpret the epitaph as a direct challenge when he sees it, for Juan appears to be dictating not only his own fate, but also what the King himself is going to do. If Juan claims—from the omniscient point of view of "death" in his epitaph—that he did not see the King for as long as he lived, he is implying, logically, that the King did not see him either. In an important essay on the popular origins of *El villano*, Marcel Bataillon describes the epitaph as a direct challenge to the King:

> Para el rey, Juan es ante todo el hombre del epitafio: éste se
> lo propone como enigma que tiene que ser descifrado, como

> dificultad que tiene que ser vencida. Toda la comedia girará
> en torno a las palabras escritas prematuramente sobre una
> lápida y a las que habrá que darles un mentís. (350)

This challenge is defined not only in terms of the proper relations between ruler and subject but also in terms of the acts of reading and interpretation.

If Juan implicitly challenges the King's authority, he also challenges that of God, for the King is often regarded as an earthly representative of the Divine order of things. The subversion implied by Juan's epitaph includes a claim to knowledge that is normally ascribed to a Divine Being:

> "ni tuvo necesidad,
> ni estuvo herido ni preso,
> ni en muchos años de edad
> vio en su casa mal suceso,
> envidia ni enfermedad."

If he does not fear any of the ills explicitly named in his epitaph and "knows" that they did not and will not happen to him before he dies, the logical implication is that Juan knows his own destiny: that he can, in effect, foresee the future. Such absolute knowledge of the future is, of course, the province of God alone. The inscription, situated in a church, therefore constitutes an implicit challenge to the authority of God. Written in stone, it has all the monumentality, all the force, of a sacred mandate: a sort of "Thou shalt not . . ." that appears to dictate limits to the powers of God and monarch. Juan's implicit denial of God has been noted by Frances Day Wardlaw:

> Through pride, the most heinous of sins, man denies his true dependence on God and credits himself for his blessings. The public of that period, accustomed to seeing the relation between subject and King as a metaphor for man's relation with God, would readily have perceived Juan's aloofness from the King as a symbol of man's rejection of God. (117)

Victor Dixon similarly considers the epitaph to be "un reto tremendo a la autoridad real, como también . . . a la Providencia divina" (289).

Throughout *El villano*, the written word appears to be an

element that is natural to the court and not to the countryside.
Juan's epitaph clearly goes contrary to this rule, but this only
serves to emphasize its odd and subversive quality. The relation that certain principal characters have with writing demonstrates this connection. Juan's daughter Lisarda, for example,
fervently aspires to courtly life and while speaking to her
suitor, Otón, proudly declares her ability to write. She explicitly includes writing among those activities that she considers
courtly: "Sé escribir, sé danzar, sé cuantas cosas / una noble
mujer en corte aprende" (1332-33). However, when Otón, a
native to the court who habitually deals with written texts of
all kinds, offers Lisarda a written promise of marriage in order
to assure her of the honesty of his intentions, she firmly
rejects it:

OTÓN:	Teneos, no os vais; que por el alto cielo que habéis de ser mujer . . .
LISARDA:	Señor, dejadme.
OTÓN:	. . . del mariscal Otón, y cumplirélo.
LISARDA:	Y, ¿qué seguro deso podéis darme?
OTÓN:	Un papel de mi mano.
LISARDA:	Y, ¿por papeles queréis que yo me atreva a aventurarme?
OTÓN:	Pues, ¿no tienen valor?
LISARDA:	El que se mira en las veletas que los aires mudan. No hay verdad en amor, todo es mentira.
	(1338-46)

Lisarda's rejection of a written guarantee is not strange or
exceptional in and of itself, yet it tantalizingly suggests the sus-
picion with which all written texts, as mere supplements
to direct face-to-face oral communication, must have been
regarded by country folk who were relatively unaccustomed to
dealing with them.[3] There are in fact many instances of written
and oral promises that go unfulfilled in the *comedia*, especially
in the context of amorous intrigues: "No hay verdad en amor,
todo es mentira." I call attention to Lisarda's ambivalent attitude toward the written word because it emphasizes her own
transition from village to courtly life and serves, of course, to
anticipate her father's.

It is interesting in this context that Lisarda responds to

Otón's verbal promise of marriage with an offering of her own: a physical object. She gives him a key by which he may enter the orchard in back of her house, in order that they might continue their conversation later: "Yo bajaré después a medianoche, / y hablaremos los dos secretamente" (1359-60). The first meeting between Lisarda and Otón in Paris had, in fact, provided something of an anticipation of this interchange. When Otón had expressed a desire to see Lisarda again, she promised that he would and then attempted to guarantee that promise by giving him a ring:

> . . . para satisfacción
> de que no os digo mentira
> (porque no sabe quien mira
> las más veces la intención),
> esta sortija tomad.
>
> (45-49)

As we shall see, Lisarda's pattern of reliance upon physical objects as a guarantee or as a temporary substitute for verbal communication anticipates Juan's own nonverbal response to written texts, that is, by way of material objects rather than in writing. She also clings to the mode of orality—the mode that is (apparently) natural to the countryside—by insisting upon *speaking* with Otón later.

The next written texts that appear in *El villano* are the letters that the King sends to Juan and that respond directly to the challenge that the epitaph constitutes. It is significant that Juan does not actually read these letters himself when he receives them. He claims to have weak eyesight and asks his son Feliciano to read them out loud to him. In this way, Juan maintains a certain distance from the King's inscribed orders. His son Feliciano, yet another aspirant to courtly life, immediately accepts the King's written words as law and his own role as reader and obeyer of that law. Juan has a certain difficulty in accepting this role, at least primarily. This is because there is still a part of him that wishes to retain his self-image as independent "king in his own corner" and as a writer of texts such as the epitaph that other people must read and obey. In her article on *El villano*, Mary Loud stresses Juan's strong sense of self-reliance:

> To go to court, to see the King, and to admit that there are
> other ways of life and persons of higher authority to whom
> he owes homage would, in Juan Labrador's mind, represent
> a lessening of his own status, and that, he refuses to contem-
> plate. He is determined to shut out any aspect of reality
> which would tend to contradict his belief in the superiority
> of his way of life and his own values. (847)

Juan appears to believe that his odd epitaph is a proof of complete self-reliance. But he *is* dependent on others, even in that
seemingly self-contained act of inscription, for the act of writing always implies that of reading: his motive for producing the
epitaph inevitably presupposes potential readers.

Juan's initial reaction to the King's letter is interesting in that
he responds physically to the written text, as though it were an
object whose sole reality consisted in its sheer material presence and not in the message that it contained. His reality clearly
lies in material objects, that is, in concrete physical presence.
He therefore places the King's letter on his head in an act of
ritual submission. Here, Juan symbolically recognizes the
King's authority and, bowing to his letter and his law, signals a
recognition of his own proper place within the social hierarchy
as subordinate to that of the actual King.

As another creator of texts, Juan Labrador does in fact have
a significant measure of kinglike authority in his own corner
of the realm. This is established throughout Acts I and II. Both
"kings," for example, arrange marriages. Yet Juan's figurative
kingdom depends completely on the true King's, for the former
is contained within the latter and is protected and maintained
by it. In Act II, for example, Feliciano tries to convince Juan to
take the opportunity to greet the King personally:

> Alegra ya tu vejez,
> hinca la rodilla en tierra
> al Rey, que con tanta guerra
> te mantiene en paz.
>
> (459-62)

Juan cannot bring himself to practice what he had earlier
preached when he claimed full allegiance to the King near the
beginning of the drama, for this would involve a conscious self-
admission that whatever pseudo royal authority he enjoys

ultimately depends upon the true king's authority and ability to maintain and uphold the law of France. This law is diffused throughout the kingdom precisely by way of such inscribed texts as the letter that Juan receives. The court is, in fact, the center of a system of culturally inscribed conventions and rules that Juan has studiously avoided all of his life and that—paradoxically—enables him to enjoy the tranquility of a private pastoral existence.

One of the villagers, Fileto, refers to the specifically ritualized dimension of courtly life, and his description is nothing less than a straight condemnation:

> cumplimientos extraños, ceremonias,
> reverencias, los cuerpos espetados,
> mucha parola, mormurar, donaires,
> risa falsa, no hacer por nadie nada,
> notable prometer, verdad ninguna,
> negar la edad y el beneficio hecho,
> deber . . . y otras cosas más sutiles. . . .
>
> (2477-83)

According to Fileto, courtly life is opposed to all sense of virtue and personal integrity, and consists largely of hypocrisy: ritualized forms of behavior that constitute an artificially intricate avoidance of, rather than a participation in, personal responsibility and productive activity. Such ritualization is eminently codified and formulaic; it is derived from and defined by a kind of "master-text." The court is characterized by a figurative form of cultural inscription that stands in marked contrast to the seemingly spontaneous, more "natural" ways of the country.

The court's intimate connection with inscription and textuality is made literal by the fact that it is specifically the more "cultivated" courtiers who make nearly all of the historical, mythological, and literary references in the drama. Along with other members of the royal party, the King reveals his erudition by making bookish references at various points throughout the drama. Immediately after reading Juan's epitaph, for example, he engages in a discussion with Otón and the Princess about the different epitaphs that they have read about and seen.

The drama's two sonnets emphasize this by virtue of their very form. The sonnet, that ever so consciously "literary" mode, is uttered by two characters, the King and Lisarda. It is most natural that the King, the quintessential cultivated man of the court, should recite a sonnet. The case of Lisarda is much more noteworthy: she has just become a lady of the court and she immediately confirms and formalizes this new status by expressing herself via the sonnet.

The two sonnets are thematically opposed to one another, and this opposition serves to highlight the intense counterpoint that characterizes the drama as a whole. The King's sonnet (2306-19) is a variation on the Horatian *Beatus ille* theme. It celebrates the tranquility of country life, especially in relation to the tribulations of life in the court, and declares the monarch's jealousy of just such a life. Citing Socrates (that is, the writings of the distant and respected past) as his authority, the King compares a life occupied in official duties with "un arroyo en tempestad airada, / que turbio y momentáneo discurría." He then compares a peaceful life with a "fuente sosegada" and ends by declaring that "Negocios a la vista son veneno. / ¡Dichoso aquel que vive como fuente, / manso, tranquilo, y de turbarse ajeno!"

Lisarda's sonnet (2706-19), on the other hand, is a celebration of the magically equalizing power of Love, which has raised her to Otón's social status and thereby enabled her to participate in courtly life:

> De grado en grado amor me va subiendo,
> que también el amor tiene su escala,
> donde ya mi bajeza a Otón iguala,
> cuya grandeza conquistar pretendo.

Like the two characters who utter them, these sonnets aspire to opposing ends. The King expresses his desire for the tranquility of a calmer pastoral existence, while Lisarda aspires to the pomp and bustle of courtly life. The "dialogue" between the two sonnets thereby embodies the essential counterpoint of *El villano*: a dialectic between the two views of life represented by the court and the village.

Another dichotomy that reinforces this counterpoint is that between the two sonnets, on the one hand, and the songs sung by the villagers, on the other. The sonnets of the court are self-conscious, "cultivated" soliloquies that give private expression to interior states of mind and spirit. (The sonnet is, of course, commonly recognized as one of the *comedia*'s principal vehicles for introspection.) The village songs, on the other hand, are simpler and more spontaneous, and they have an explicitly social function. They are sung in unison—not alone—by the villagers or by a group of musicians and convey popular, communal themes. One appears near the beginning of Act II: "A caza va el caballero / por los montes de París" (1252-53). Another, almost tribal in tone, is the work song that accompanies the villagers' harvest at the start of Act III: "Deja las avellanicas, moro, / que yo me las vareare" (2069-70). The mood of these songs is festive and their concern is with concrete actions and objects rather than with the introspective world of thoughts and emotions.[4] The dichotomy between sonnets and songs exists on the formal level as well. The village songs are in *octosílabos*, the meter that best represents the popular and communal (oral) mode of the medieval *cantares de gesta* and the *romances*. The sonnets are, of course, in *endecasílabos* and, perhaps most self-consciously of all verse forms, represent—from Dante and Petrarch on down—the "cultivated" and specifically *written* literary tradition of Renaissance humanism.

There are five soliloquies in *El villano*: a long recitation by Juan Labrador in Act I, celebrating the *Beatus ille* theme (350-424); soon after this, Feliciano's brief plaint about his father Juan's refusal to go see the King (537-50); a short meditation by the King in Act II (1540-63); and the King's and Lisarda's sonnets in Act III (2306-19; 2706-19). In this drama the soliloquy has strong associations with courtly life. Although the court is where institutional, symbolic public presence such as that of the King is enacted, it is also the place where individuals most separate themselves from one another in a strictly personal sense. It is paradoxically true that the place where the most people congregate—the court—is precisely where the social and cultural differences between them become most apparent. Such stratification, the very base of society, is defined by and diffuses from the court (Hesse, "Sociology" 36-40). The social hierarchy is therefore determined according to the same models that we have been examining throughout, those of presence and absence. This does not deny that such public figures as a king are also, in an institutional sense, more "present" to society at large than anyone else. The higher a person is on the

31

social ladder, the more present he or she is, in a strictly civic sense. The price of such civic presence, however, is the deferral of the private self, which emerges only at rare and secret moments. The sonnets and other soliloquies in *El villano* give voice to these moments of courtly privacy and introspection.

Juan's soliloquy in Act I, therefore, aids in establishing the pseudo royalty that he enjoys within his own corner of the kingdom. His discursive "absence" from others parallels that of the King. However, the King's absence differs from Juan's in the following important way: it is this absenting of the private self that enables any king to be functionally, institutionally "present" in all the corners of the kingdom. Juan partakes of no such broad institutional or societal existence, except within the confines of his own private realm. His whole life has been, in fact, a studied avoidance of such civic presence.

If the court is essentially a world that is governed by a rigid set of cultural inscriptions (laws, rules, institutions), then the village and countryside basically contain "things": the natural world of physical, tangible reality (Zamora Vicente xxxiv). I have already suggested that the epitaph is seemingly half-text and half-thing, and that Juan's primary reaction to the King's first letter is more physical than textual. In the same way, his response to the letter is not verbal but physical: like Lisarda, he "speaks" by way of objects. Along with the money that the King has requested as a loan from him, Juan Labrador sends a lamb with a knife tied around its neck. As Juan himself later explains, these objects express his humility before the King and his beginning sense of self-sacrifice to the common good. Bruce Wardropper has written convincingly on the motif of private sacrifice for the sake of public good:

> . . . si la felicidad del reino entero depende del amor entre el monarca y sus súbditos, el precio que paga el individuo no es demasiado subido. Juan Labrador resulta ser la víctima propiciatoria que envió éste simbólicamente al Rey. Se le sacrifica a él por el bienestar del cuerpo público. ("La venganza" 771)

It is through contact with the King—disguised as Dionís—that Juan begins the transition from (overly) private citizen to public servant. As José Antonio Maravall has noted:

> Es necesaria . . . la aproximación al rey y la entrada en el alrededor de la gracia real que es la nobleza, para llevar a plenitud, para perfeccionar una condición personal en su grado más elevado. Frente a la tesis . . . que en un principio expone el labrador . . . "Reyes los que viven son / del trabajo de sus manos," . . . la doctrina de Lope, siguiendo las finalidades de la comedia, se resume en que la superior condición del hombre está en insertarse plenamente en la sociedad monárquico-aristocrático y no quedar marginado. (121-22)

It is interesting to note in *El villano* that, as functioning ruler, the King depends upon various modes of absence in order to make his institutional presence felt throughout the kingdom. For example, he first visits Juan in disguise, under the pseudonym of Dionís, thus "absenting" himself while enjoying a secret presence. Later on, of course, he sends written letters to Juan: yet another "absential" form of communication. The King utilizes the mode of absence in order to function as an institution, that is, as a symbol. It is, paradoxically, by way of such absential means that ethical presence in the form of full civic responsibility is finally imposed upon Juan. The price of public participation is, as we have seen, a partial denial of the private self.

It is the epitaph at the beginning of the drama that sets the pattern for Juan's peculiarly physical relationship with written texts. His gravestone/epitaph is a metaphor for his own existence: he has shaped and inscribed that stone in much the same way that he has ordered and shaped the kingdom of his own *rincón*. The image is most fitting, for the stone is literally a piece of that "corner." The role of the villager, it seems, is truly that of *labrador*: to deal physically and by labor of hand with the raw material of the natural world and thereby to impose order upon it. The role of a king, on the other hand, is to impose an abstract, institutional order upon all of the corners of the realm, and not by physical, but rather, by textual or inscriptional means: decrees, mandates, laws.

Juan's epitaph has a pointedly physical existence that stands in marked contrast to the abstract texts of the King. It has a stony solidity, a "here and now" that is the mark of the private citizen. Those texts that the King produces as governing institution have no here and now, at least not in the same sense.

They are not confined to physical space; they are not inscribed on stone. Rather, they are examples of cultural inscription that function publicly, not privately, by way of their dissemination throughout the entire kingdom. The King's texts function by virtue of their relative nondependence upon physicality, by force of their institutional authority. Their more figurative presence does not radically depend, as does Juan's epitaph, upon their physical reality; they are forms of inscription rather than examples of mere writing. The epitaph, on the other hand, is literally confined to the here and now, nailed to the stone of presence that is Juan Labrador's corner. Although the epitaph is inscribed, it has, paradoxically, many of the characteristics of oral speech. As such, Juan's words have no power beyond his own immediate and personal existence, despite his belief to the contrary, and the whole enterprise of the King, in this drama, is that of proving this to him. The sheer physicality of Juan's epitaph serves to limit its influence to that of thoroughly private citizen.

If, in *El villano*, the *things* of the countryside stand in contrast to the *texts* of the court, then those texts that do appear in the countryside take on special meaning: the King's discovery and reading of Juan's epitaph, for example, is the origin of the drama's main action. By the same token, those physical objects that appear in court also gain in significance. I refer specifically to the scepter, mirror, and sword that the King shows to Juan in the final and blatantly ceremonial scene. These things take on meaning both explicitly, because of the King's explanation of them, and implicitly, in the relation that they have with the gravestone/epitaph with which the primary plot begins. These final objects—scepter, mirror, and sword—are infused with meaning, with "text": they have meanings aside from the primary pragmatic uses to which they are conventionally put. The drama appears to illustrate, self-referentially, the process whereby cultural or institutional symbols evolve. *Symbol* is almost consciously defined in *El villano* as a material object that is infused with meaning or *text*.

This casts an interesting light on the gravestone/epitaph and the process whereby it takes on meaning. It is a primarily natural object: a stone that has been artificially shaped and then inscribed with a text on its front. It serves as a contrast to those objects that appear in the court at the end of the drama. The scepter, mirror, and sword are "completed" symbols, objects that have implicit meanings that may be spelled out, if necessary and as the King does.[5] They are, in effect, texts that are not explicitly written out. It is significant that these final objects are much more consciously artificial and further removed from the world of nature that supplied their raw materiality. They are finished products: more drastically, more completely developed as symbols. They are the endpoint as well as the counterpoint of the process begun by Juan's gravestone. In this drama, *text* or *meaning* is shown as explicit and denaturalized in the village, implicit and naturalized in the court. In enacting the dichotomy between village and court, between the gravestone and the more finely elaborate objects of the final scene, between explicit and implicit texts, *El villano* points up the relation between thing and symbol. It dramatizes the process by which culture imposes meaning and order upon the raw phenomena of life.

If Juan Labrador represents the kingdom at large (the natural countryside, "raw material"), then it is the King and the surrounding court that finally infuses those raw forms with meaning, "textualizes" them. Text is determined, literally, by context, and Juan's context has radically changed when the drama ends. So, therefore, has his meaning as a character. He has paradoxically died the death that was prefigured by his epitaph and that is later confirmed by his own words when he reveals to the King in the final scene that he had feared to face him because he felt that such a confrontation might cause his death: "me pareció que solamente el verte / pudiera ser la causa de mi muerte" (2790-91). His greatest fear has come true: seeing the King has, in fact, caused his "death," but it is a symbolic one that has resulted in his rebirth as Juan "Cortesano."[6]

The new Juan is different from the old in that he has civic responsibility. As I have said, there is a sense in which Juan truly is a type of king at the beginning of the drama. Within his limited corner, he has many of a king's privileges, but none of his responsibilities: "Yo tengo en este rincón / no sé qué de rey también; / mas duermo y como más bien" (1669-71). Indeed, village life is portrayed in *El villano* as being more or less free from worries and cares. For example, the King makes his first appearance in the countryside while on his way to go hunting, that is, to indulge in an exercise of leisure. Throughout the

Western classical tradition, hunting has always been regarded as a particularly kingly form of entertainment because it is a sportive and playful simulacrum of the serious business of waging war. Hunting is the monarchy's *otium*, while war is its *negotium*. By emphasizing this dichotomy so explicitly at the beginning of the drama and with such direct reference to the King, the archetypically pastoral ("escapist") dimensions of Juan Labrador's native environment are also underlined. The King must go out into the countryside in order to divert himself temporarily from courtly responsibilities; but the countryside is precisely where Juan lives habitually, and it is this that inspires the King's envy.

When the King goes in disguise to visit Juan in Act II, dinner is served to accompanying music that is sung by local musicians. Like the King's sonnet, their song is a variation on the Horatian *Beatus ille* and is part of the *menosprecio de corte, alabanza de aldea* tradition that found such a variety of expression throughout the Spanish Golden Age:

> ¡Cuán bienaventurado
> aquel puede llamarse justamente,
> que, sin tener cuidado
> de la malicia y lengua de la gente
> a la virtud contraria,
> la suya pasa en vida solitaria!
>   Caliéntase el enero
> alrededor de sus hijuelos todos,
> a un roble ardiendo entero,
> y allí contando de diversos modos
> de la extranjera guerra,
> duerme seguro y goza de su tierra.
>
> (1865-76)

The grim realities—the *negotium* aspect—of war are distanced in the second stanza ("la extranjera guerra") and made into a form of *otium* that, as entertainment, parallels the earlier hunting activity of the King: stories told for diversion by the fireside among the villagers, who can sleep safely and who securely enjoy the fruits of their lands.

The King jealously recognizes that Juan's whole life consists of this idyllic and carefree existence, and thus the monarch forces him to submit ultimately to a life of responsible service at the court. In fact, it is precisely the King's perception of Juan's nonparticipation in the life of public duty that causes the monarch to hold up his alter ego, Dionís, as an example to Juan of what a good citizen does in service to his king. There has been little critical speculation about the King's choice of "Dionís" as a pseudonym during his visit to Juan's home. Interestingly, there was a Portuguese king named Dionís (b. 1261-d. 1325) who was known as "el Rey Labrador." Could the King in *El villano* be slyly implying that he is much worthier than Juan of the title *labrador* because he, as functioning monarch, has all of the responsibilities, while his subject apparently has none?

The following dialogue occurs when the King makes his appearance—in disguise—at Juan's house:

> JUAN: ¿Qué nombre tenéis?
> REY: Dionís.
> JUAN: ¿Qué oficio o qué dignidad?
> REY: Alcaide de la ciudad
>   y los muros de París.
> JUAN: Nunca tal oficio oí.
> REY: Es merced que el Rey me ha hecho,
>   por heridas que en el pecho,
>   sirviéndole, recibí.
>
> (1608-15)

As someone who daily serves in the presence of the King and who has received wounds while serving him in the grim *negotium* of war, Dionís is everything that Juan is not: the exemplary civil servant whose life consists of public duty. Dionís is, in fact, the direct contradiction of everything that Juan claims to have been in his epitaph:

> "Yace aquí Juan Labrador,
> que nunca sirvió a señor,
> ni vio la corte, ni al Rey,
> . . . .
> ni estuvo herido ni preso. . . ."

The relation between Juan Labrador and the new Juan is analogous to that between the gravestone and the refined, more artificial objects of the final scene. Both Juan Labrador and his gravestone/epitaph are "unfinished" and in a seminatural state, while Juan "Cortesano" and the scepter, mirror, and sword are fully developed and purified symbols of the courtly life and influence that gives them their meaning and their existence.

The only place in the countryside where written texts are normally found is the church, which is where Juan's epitaph is discovered. It is interesting that the King makes his first appearance here, for the church is, in a certain sense, an extension of many of the same motifs that are associated with the court: it is one other place that disseminates cultural inscriptions that serve to define, determine, and give order to reality. Juan is ultimately subordinated to the order constituted by God and King. The man who does not wish to submit directly (in full presence of the King) to the social order has to observe it, finally, according to the pattern of life that best seems to represent the countryside: the same model of *presence*, a presence that is paradoxically constituted by thoroughly social modes of inscription. Ironically, absolute physical presence manifests itself in Juan's final destiny, for both he and his family will live out the rest of their lives in full presence of and service to the King. This ultimate presence is officially confirmed by an example of the model of absence: the King's written decree in the final scene authoritatively confirms their permanent and mutual presence, and contradicts absolutely the epitaph with which the main intrigue begins.

El villano thus dramatizes an inversion of the original relation between Juan Labrador and his king. Juan is converted from his self-appointed "kingly" role as absent writer of texts to that of ever-present recipient of the King's direct *oral* orders. At the same time, the King has undergone a transition from recipient and reader of Juan's original inscribed text (the epitaph) to producer of direct, oral orders that will be carried out by Juan in his new role as *mayordomo*. Revolving around the oppositional axis of written and spoken communication, *El villano* demonstrates their ultimate interdependence.

The drama's action is, in effect, an extended chiasmus that manifests how orality is an inevitable part of the written word and how various modes of cultural inscription underlie even the most ostensibly pure forms of orality. As Paul Julian Smith has stated in reference to Lope's *Peribáñez*, ". . . 'natural' orality is preceded by a complex cultural inscription" (136). Juan's use of objects from his native environment—the lamb with the knife tied around its neck—to speak symbolically to the King proves that even the villager's discourse is thoroughly compromised by pre-established and conventional codes of meaning. Derrida refers to the chiasmus in his discussion of the written word's portrayal as a *pharmakon* in Plato's *Phaedrus*:

> If the *pharmakon* is "ambivalent," it is because it constitutes the medium in which opposites are opposed, the movement and the play that links them among themselves, reverses them or makes one side cross over into the other (soul/body, good/evil, inside/outside, memory/forgetfulness, speech/ writing, etc.). ("Plato's" 127)

Juan Labrador and the King are, finally, interdependent: inevitably involved in one another and mutually defining, as are the ways of life that they exemplify, that of the village and that of the court (Dixon 294). Paul Julian Smith makes a similar observation about the apparent opposition of town and country in *Peribáñez*:

> the island of peasant idyll (such as it is) is entirely surrounded by the ocean of noble influence . . . the town/ country dichotomy is founded not on true "opposites" in the logical sense, but on "relatives": mutually defining or dialectical terms. The paradigm functions only as a cultural inscription always already in place; and the mutual dependence of town and country underlies both social practice and dramatic text. (138)

In the modern world, at least, any form of order—be it social, cultural, religious, or political—depends upon the model of absence, i.e., inscription:

> Political decentralization, dispersion, and decentering of sovereignty calls, paradoxically, for the existence of a capital, a center of usurpation and of substitution. In opposition to the autarchic cities of Antiquity, which were their own centers and conversed in the living voice, the modern capital is always a monopoly of writing. It commands by written laws, decrees, and literature. (Derrida, *Grammatology* 302)

This is true because of the simple fact that the structuring, governing organism can no longer be physically present in all the corners of the kingdom. It imposes itself, rather, by way of institutional, symbolic presence. This notion is reinforced explicitly by the King himself, who comes full circle in the final scene of *El villano* by borrowing a metaphor from the natural (not the artificial) world to express the monarchy's omnipresence:

> Mira al Rey, Juan Labrador;
> que no hay rincón tan pequeño
> adonde no alcance el sol.
> Rey es el sol.
>
> (2906-09)

The organism that imposes order remains outside of the present moment in order to be able to control it, to characterize and define it, in order to give it a sense of its own destiny. This structuring organism creates and disseminates cultural inscriptions—customs, laws, "history"—that the structured body reads and obeys, interpreting according to present necessities, that is, within the flux of the present moment and in on-going life. Culture—the soul of perception—cannot exist, however, without the living body that lends its form, that interprets it. The kingdom at large, culture's living form, is composed of many Juan Labradores and lives in the present moment, but that present moment is dictated and prescribed by the model of absence: the inscriptions of civilization itself. The written word in *El villano en su rincón* serves, therefore, to symbolize the process by which culture defines itself, imposing order on reality, that is, the process by which *things* are infused with *texts* that no longer need be written. Lope's play dramatizes the very process of civilization: the evolution from explicit to implicit text, from thing to symbol, from nature to culture. But the movement between these oppositions is by no means uni-directional nor is it absolute. The essential dialectic of *El villano* insures the openendedness of this mutually defining process, which, by its very nature (not to say its culture), is unending.

Chapter Two

Presence and Absence in
La estrella de Sevilla

Critics have often complained that much of the attention devoted to *La estrella de Sevilla* (1623) has been concerned almost exclusively with the question of authorship, despite the fact that it has long been considered one of the "gems" of Golden Age drama.[1] This situation has changed with the appearance of several articles devoted to formal and thematic aspects of the play itself. One of the most suggestive and insightful of these is Elias L. Rivers's "The Shame of Writing in *La estrella de Sevilla*" (1980), which, as its title indicates, deals specifically with the function of writing. My aim in this chapter is to examine once again the written texts that appear in *La estrella* and to consider what is their dramatic function and their relation to the so called honor code.

La estrella's action begins when King Sancho ("el Bravo") of Castile conceives a passion for Estrella Tavera, one of many women who have come out to welcome him to Seville. The King repeatedly attempts to gain access to Estrella by offering bribes to her brother Busto. When Busto repeatedly refuses to betray his sister, who is already engaged to be married to Sancho Ortiz, the monarch finally gains illicit entry by bribing Natilde, a slave girl. Busto arrives unexpectedly, however, and challenges the King, who, concealing himself with a cloak, manages to escape. When Busto confirms Natilde's complicity, he executes her publicly by hanging her outside the palace walls. Swearing vengeance, the King orders Sancho Ortiz to carry out the secret execution of a purported traitor and gives him two papers: one containing the name of the "traitor" and the other, a full and unconditional pardon. Sancho refuses the written pardon, claiming that the King's oral promise to pardon him is sufficient. He is, of course, shocked when he reads his future brother-in-law's name on the other piece of paper, but reluctantly keeps his word by publicly challenging Busto and then killing him in a fair fight.

By carrying out the King's order so openly, Sancho provokes his own immediate capture and imprisonment by the authorities. When Sancho refuses to reveal his motives, the King, who wishes to spare Sancho's life without revealing his own complicity, orders him placed in Estrella's custody and punished at her discretion. Under cover of a cape, she immediately frees him, but when Sancho learns the identity of his benefactor, he insists on returning to prison. Again faced with the prospect of admitting responsibility for Busto's execution, the King requests that the local magistrates sentence Sancho to exile rather than death. When they refuse, the King hastily arranges Estrella's betrothal to a Castilian prince, requesting that she publicly pardon Sancho. She does so, but the magistrates insist upon carrying out Sancho's death sentence in the name of justice. The King has no choice, finally, but to take full public responsibility for Busto's death and to absolve Sancho. Estrella and Sancho realize that they could no longer live happily together as husband and wife, given all that has occurred, and the drama ends with their final separation.

La estrella's action consists of two plots that are causally connected: the final action of the first, Sancho's killing of Busto, is also the initial action of the second. Both plots involve a confrontation, based upon the question of personal honor, between the King and one of his subjects, but whereas the first ends in death, the second one barely avoids this conclusion when the citizens of Seville bring the King to an awareness of their honor and force him to live up to that ideal as their ruler.

Rivers's study of *La estrella* emphasizes the fact that the play is essentially a dramatization of conflicts engendered by the traditional code of personal honor. This code governs all sexual and social relations and is dependent upon presence, which is the necessary prerequisite to oral communication: "Feelings of honor and shame function only when people can face and talk to one another orally; only under such circumstances of physical presence are there genuine speech acts, honorable obligations, or shameful losses of face" (115). It follows, Rivers tells us, that written communication tends to subvert the traditional honor code, for it functions by way of absence: the act of writing is always private, spatially and temporally removed from the equally private act of reading, and in that respect "liberates" the author from responsibility for its contents.

What is the relation between the honor code and morality in *La estrella de Sevilla* and how does that relation function? The term *honor code* has raised more questions than it has answered because there continues to be great disagreement about its meaning and function.[2] Most critics have focused on its essentially social character, as does Margaret Wilson:

> This unwritten but fetish-like code regulated all social relationships: those between king and subject, between superior and inferior, between friend and friend, and between members of the same family. Its basis is the paramount importance of the right ordering of social relationships. The wholeness, or integrity of society comes before personal integrity; in fact the latter can scarcely be thought of apart from the former. The criterion of behaviour is thus always a social one: not so much to be, as to be seen to be. Honour resides not in the ordering of one's life, but in the esteem in which one is held by others. (43)

There is no question but that the honor code is, in great part, a social mechanism: a means of imposing and maintaining order. As such, the monarch is its focal point: "The king, as the head of society, is the embodiment and fount of honour" (44). Gustavo Correa similarly tells us that "El rey era el máximo portador de honra y sus actos en relación con sus súbditos conferían honra" ("El doble" 100). This is exemplified by many Golden Age dramas. *La estrella de Sevilla*, however, dramatizes a clear exception to this rule, for, although the verb *honrar* is most frequently associated with King Sancho, this association is always highly ironic. As part of a consistent pattern of linguistic and social subversion, his public act of *honrar* inevitably translates into *deshonrar* on the personal level.

In contrast to the King's subversive *honrar*, the word *honor* is most frequently associated with Busto Tavera and, later on, with Sancho Ortiz. Likewise, the text highlights Busto's strong sense of justice by its pointed rhyming of his name with the word *justo* the first time that he is mentioned (166-67) and consistently throughout. The drama thus appears insistently to oppose two types of honor: a purely social type that is described by Wilson (above) and a type of personal honor that may be identified with a sense of individual achievement, integrity, and virtue. In a fine essay on *La estrella*, J. L. Brooks differentiates between these two types of honor by calling them, respectively, *honra* and *honor*:

> In the play, as in the *comedia* in general, of course, the two words are used indiscriminately to express the concept of *honor* as it was used by the dramatists, but there seems to be a clear cut distinction between the two ideas. Whereas to the king the outward—*lo que dirán*—in other words, *honra*, is what matters, to Busto and Sancho it is virtue, the inner quality of goodness, or *honor*, that is all important. (11-12)

Brooks conceives of *honra* in *La estrella* as exterior and social; *honor*, on the other hand, is interior, personal, and has a specifically moral basis: "the inner quality of goodness."

Such a morally based concept of honor is clearly related to Alexander A. Parker's well-known application of the principle of "poetic justice" (". . . that wrongdoing should not go 'unpunished' and that virtue should not go 'unrewarded'") to the *comedia* ("Spanish" 687). Within the context of poetic justice, the two types of honor *do* have a specifically moral value: *honra* is the "just" reward, the outer and social recognition, of one who lives and acts with inner, personal *honor*. In Saussurean terms, we might describe this relation by saying that *honra* is a kind of motivated "signifier" to *honor*, its "signified." It is clear that *La estrella*'s King Sancho consistently utilizes public *honra* in order to subvert personal *honor*, both his own and that of his subjects. The play dramatizes, therefore, the radical disjunction of this ideally motivated connection between *honra* and *honor*, and it is precisely from this disjunction that *La estrella* derives much of its tragic force.

The problem with this conception, however, is that it often oversimplifies the drama. Brooks states, for example, that Busto and Sancho do not care about the social dimension of honor: "At no stage does either Busto or Sancho show any interest in what people may say about them" (12). It is clear, however, that they do. (It would be very strange if they did not:

we are, after all, dealing with a *comedia*.) In Act I, for example, Busto protests against the King's expressed desire to enter his house, precisely because of the social implications:

> en casa
> tengo una hermosa doncella
> solamente, que la caso
> ya con escrituras hechas,
> y *no sonará muy bien*
> *en Sevilla, cuando sepan*
> *que a visitarla venís.*
>
> (715-21)

Sancho Ortiz also cares about his reputation, that is, his sense of social honor. When the King orders him to carry out the execution, the monarch advises that it be done when the victim is unprepared ("descuidado") for it (1527-28), but Sancho rejects this advice, not only on moral grounds, but also because of its social implications:

> . . . al que mata y no pelea,
> nadie puede disculpalle;
>   y gana más el que muere
> a traición, que el que le mata;
> *que el muerto opinión adquiere,*
> *y el vivo, con cuantos trata*
> *su alevosía refiere.*
>
> (1535-41)

Nevertheless, it is also clear that Busto and Sancho believe social honor, or *opinión*, to be without value unless it is motivated by a strong sense of virtue. Busto expresses this belief just prior to his death:

> Habréis en mí conocido
> sangre, nobleza y valor,
> y *virtud, que es el honor*;
> *que sin ella honor no ha habido. . . .*
>
> (1801-04)

Therefore, although the question of *honra* and *honor* is not quite so clear-cut as Brooks apparently presumes, the gist of his argument is certainly valid: Busto and Sancho do essentially represent honor that is based upon morality.

This ideally motivated relation between *honra* and *honor* might also be described, in Derridean terms, as a "metaphysics of honor," according to which *honra* is the outer sign and therefore the potentially distorting *supplement* of "pure" *honor*. This, of course, is the same relation that Derrida has posited as a part of the Western metaphysical tradition's logocentric concept of writing: its status as secondary, deformative, and subversive, by virtue of its dependence upon absence. The spoken word, by virtue of its dependence upon presence, is seen as pure and unmediated.[3]

The metaphysics of presence is literalized and championed by the action of *La estrella de Sevilla,* for the King effectively dishonors the citizens of Seville by way of the supplement to oral communication, that absential and mediated means, written texts. His *honra* is thus intimately associated with writing. The written word's inherent absence enables him to function in secrecy and to subordinate his social role as monarch to personal desires. As Rivers points out, this orientation toward writing and absence threatens the essentially oral basis of *honor*:

> The written contract, as a substitute speech act, destroys the honor system itself, which depends upon the non-reiterable uniqueness of the performative utterance. A man may sign his name after he raises his right hand and swears; but, from a traditional point of view, that signature is an inadequate substitute for the authentic oral performative utterance, pronounced face to face. . . . Notaries are invented as witnesses to supplement with their signatures the written traces of a speech act, but what remains is only paper, "que lo aguanta todo," without the honor identified with the unique act and presence of flesh and blood. When a man is judged in terms of a fixed written law code, we can safely say that the traditional oral system of personal honor is dead. ("Shame" 115-16)

Honor, as opposed to *honra,* is manifested by way of orality and is dependent upon what might be called "moral presence." In this sense, *La estrella* dramatizes a reversal of the values with which written texts are portrayed in *El villano en su rincón.* In Lope's drama, the King's writing functions as a governing force, a means of imposing order. In *La estrella,* on the other hand, the King uses writing to accomplish his own private purposes and thereby to undermine the social and ethical order.

The first reference to written texts in *La estrella* occurs when Don Arias attempts to convince the monarch to honor Busto in order to seduce his sister:

> Si tú le das y él recibe,
> se obliga; y si es obligado,
> pagará lo que le has dado;
> que al que dan, en bronce escribe.
>
> (201-04)

The obligation that Don Arias is talking about involves the honorable acceptance of a favor and the feeling of gratitude that conventionally accompanies it. His invoking of this principle is most cynical, for he claims that by obliging Busto, the King will be able to get what he wants, namely, Estrella. The counselor is contemptuous of any dimension of personal honor or integrity that might be connected with such a transaction and expresses his attitude toward obligation in coldly mercantile terms: "pagará lo que le has dado." Indeed, he hopes that this cynical abuse of the principle of obligation will allow the King to *dishonor* Busto by the seduction of his sister, rather than to *honor* him. This is only the beginning of a pattern of explicit linguistic corruption—a radical disjunction between signifieds and their conventionally assigned signifiers—that is enacted by Don Arias and the King throughout the drama, whereby such terms as *obligation* and *honor* take on meanings that are radically different from or even opposed to what they originally signified.

The counselor invokes the authority of the principle of obligations by claiming that they are "written in bronze." Bronze is a material that, because of its hardness and durability, is traditionally associated with the erection of public statues and monuments. As Rivers notes, whatever is written in bronze cannot be forgotten or erased from public memory ("Shame" 107). The specifically public function of bronze highlights the subversive nature of Don Arias's advice: although his "en bronce escribe" is deliberately metaphorical in nature, his invocation of its public authority is most ironic in that he wishes to use it to effect purely private and illicit ends. The theme of dishonor is thereby connected with the concept of writing from the very start of the drama.

By endowing its object of reference with a kind of immortality, inscription in bronze is, of course, inevitably associated with the memory of a culture: its sense of public history.[4] From the very beginning of *La estrella*, in fact, King Sancho is patently aware of his "historical" status as a public ruler: ". . . con prósperas fortunas / haré que de mí se acuerde" (39-40). The irony here consists in the fact that King Sancho will be remembered, but not in the way that he would like to be. The various references throughout *La estrella* to inscription in bronze inevitably carry just such historical connotations.[5]

Written texts make their first onstage appearance very early in the drama, when the King receives two written petitions. (Just as in *El villano en su rincón*, an intimate relation between the King and the written word is immediately established: in Lope's play, we remember, the King's first act is to read Juan Labrador's epitaph.) The two men who present these documents, Gonzalo de Ulloa and Fernán Pérez de Medina, have both come to petition King Sancho for the same military post, the command of forces stationed on the frontier of Archidona. The contrast between the two documents—and that between the two men who have brought them—is immediately apparent: Gonzalo bases his petition on the past services of his father, recently deceased, who had held the position for fourteen years (336-37); Fernán, on the other hand, bases his petition on his own services as a soldier for the last twenty (340-56). The petitions embody the two types of honor discussed above: honor that has been inherited as a result of social status and honor that has been earned and that derives from personal accomplishment.

Despite having two eligible candidates for the position, the King wishes to award it to Busto and asks him to give an oral recounting of his past accomplishments (357). Busto can think of no military service that he has performed and requests only that justice be administered in the decision:

> Dar este oficio es justicia
> a uno de los dos aquí;

que si me lo dais a mí,
hacéis, señor, injusticia.

(377-80)

Busto's strong sense of fairness is further emphasized when,
unlike Gonzalo de Ulloa (who attempts to "cash in" on his
father's services), he rejects the type of honor that has been
inherited:

Referir de mis pasados
los soberanos blasones,
tantos vencidos pendones
y castillos conquistados,
pudiera; pero, señor,
ya por ellos merecieron
honor; y si ellos sirvieron,
no merezco yo su honor.

(361-68)

Busto sides with honor that has been "earned" when he advises
that the post be given to Fernán Pérez de Medina, based upon
the latter's own accomplishments and life:

Y si va a decir verdad,
Fernán Pérez de Medina
merece el cargo; que es dina
de la frontera su edad.

(385-88)

He appeals, finally, to the King's sense of fairness:

Sólo quiero (y la razón
y la justicia lo quieren)
darles a los que sirvieren
debida satisfacción.

(393-96)

The King, however, offers Busto the position in order to have
more ready access to his sister. The monarch's method of oper-
ating is therefore anything but just and is especially ironic in
relation to the wisdom and the sense of fairness that is exemplified by Busto's response. This first encounter between
Busto and the monarch thus establishes an explicit opposition

between them precisely in terms of *lo justo* and *gusto*.[6] Whereas Busto is the embodiment of justice and honor, the King (who *should* be their embodiment) acts to undercut their linguistic and institutional value. Their abuse is the means by which he accomplishes their opposites, injustice and dishonor, in order to satisfy private motivations (*gusto*). Inés Azar has succinctly described this situation:

> As an institutional figure, a King is a model of perfect subordination of self to social context, of private concerns to public obligations. But King Sancho is a corrupt King precisely because he subordinates the social system to his personal desires and the public good to his private passions. (5)

Estrella Tavera mentions written texts when she attempts to ease Sancho Ortiz's concern about possible obstacles to their marriage: "hechas las escrituras / tan firmes y seguras, / el casamiento es llano" (556-58). Sancho remains uneasy despite her attempt to reassure him, for he cannot bring himself to believe in written words as a guarantee. This is the beginning of a sustained criticism of written communication by Sancho, a criticism that will become much more explicit in Acts II and III. Considering the events that are to occur, his distrust of the written word is perfectly justified, for, despite Busto's persistent invoking of the written contracts that purportedly guarantee it (643-46; 717-18; 1791-92), Sancho Ortiz's marriage to Estrella never takes place. The action of *La estrella* appears in this way consistently to deny the ostensible authority of written documents, like contracts or signatures, that are, according to the traditional code of personal honor, "inadequate substitute[s] for the authentic oral performative utterance, pronounced face to face" (Rivers, "Shame" 115).

Another written text, the order with which the King bribes Natilde, is very important from a functional standpoint; the King's act of issuing this document helps to set up all of the action that follows. It also illustrates the institutional power of texts written by the King to contain, to give, and to take away such abstract notions as freedom: "éste es, mujer, el papel, / con la *libertad* en él" (922-23). Mandates issued by a king have immediate and public effects and have all the weight of officialdom and royal authority behind them. The document ordering Natilde's freedom has all this, but because the King's motivations for issuing it are private rather than public and dishonorable rather than honorable, it is issued in secrecy. By acting secretly in this way, the King not only ignores the social order which is conventionally maintained by such written documents, but also undercuts the public functioning of *cédulas* themselves as an institution.

Despite its conventionally public function, the King's *cédula* ordering freedom for Natilde is the *private* contradiction of those "escrituras . . . firmes y seguras" that purport to guarantee the wedding between Sancho Ortiz and Estrella. The King contradicts those written contracts with another written document that is motivated, not by institutional desire for the public good, but by personal (i.e., sexual) desire. Symbolized by the contradiction of these two written texts is the tension inherent in any monarchy, that is, the battle between the King's "two bodies": the governing institution and the living, breathing man. I refer, of course, to that widespread medieval doctrine, exhaustively studied by Ernst Kantorowicz, whereby it was held that the monarch had, in effect, two bodies, one "natural" (personal) and the other "corporate" (the office), and that the social order and the well-being of the state depended upon the subordination of the former to the latter.[7] The written order of Natilde's freedom is also the first positive proof of the moral corruption of the King. This corruption is already evident in the illicit methods by which he attempts to seduce Estrella, but the document constitutes material evidence that is there for Busto and the inhabitants of Seville, after him, to see.

By using written texts to give orders, King Sancho is able to maintain himself in absence and thereby to avoid (temporarily) owning up to his acts; the drama thus draws an implicit analogy between presence and moral responsibility. Interestingly, the King remains figuratively absent, even when he is physically present. When he enters Busto's house, for example, he does so secretly, making sure beforehand that its owner will be absent. He enters under the protective covering of a cape so as to avoid recognition by all except Natilde, the slave girl. When Busto unexpectedly confronts him, the King claims from beneath his cape that he has come to Busto's house in order to honor him (1001-05). Busto, of course, emphatically denies the validity of this claim:

> . . . si mi honor procuráis,
> ¿cómo embozado venís?
> Honrándome ¿os encubrís?
> dándome honor ¿os tapáis?
>
> (1009-12)

Busto argues that true honor consists in the responsibility implied by open and public presence. His words throughout this scene serve, in fact, to emphasize that the King *must* be absent, for the anonymous intruder's behavior could never be that of a true king. When the intruder insists that he is the King, Busto expresses incredulity:

> Es engaño.
> ¡El Rey procurar mi daño,
> solo, embozado, y sin gente?
> No puede ser; y a su Alteza
> aquí, villano, ofendes,
> pues defeto en él ponéis,
> que es una extraña bajeza.
> ¿El Rey había de estar
> sus vasallos ofendiendo?
>
> (1022-30)

Busto emphasizes that the intruder's absential and secretive manner ("solo, embozado, y sin gente") is radically opposed to the self-consciously public manner of a true king. Even further, the fact that the King *names* himself without actually emerging from beneath his cloak serves to make manifest the radical disjunction between his public self, manifested by his uttered words, and his private, interior self. His disembodied voice directly contradicts the acts that his body had attempted to commit.

Busto's reaction—his public hanging of Natilde with the King's order of freedom in her hand—is a direct refutation of that written order and, at the same time, a raising of the stakes from the private realm to the public one. As William C. McCrary states: "what hitherto had been a private conflict involving two individuals now becomes a matter of state" (509). The King has already dishonored Busto by entering his house without permission. The monarch has transgressed the principle of the inviolability of personal property, just as he did by bribing Busto's slave (yet another piece of personal property) and by attempting the seduction of his sister, a woman he knows to be promised to another man in marriage. The King has thus denied Busto's personal integrity, his status, and his authority as an individual: the King, in short, has denied him his honor.

By putting the order in the hand of the dead Natilde, Busto has radically changed its original communicative context (to say the least). Instead of the liberty that had been promised to her by Don Arias and the King, Natilde receives nothing other than death, which serves here as a contrary to that promised liberty. In this context, therefore, Busto refutes the King's power: he sends an unwritten communication, telling him, in effect, that a royal order of this type is nothing more than "dead letter." This image of the dead and suspended slave girl, with the note in her hand, is a gruesome contrary to the unwritten "letter" that Juan Labrador sends to his king in *El villano en su rincón*. In Lope's play, Juan responds to the King's written petition to borrow some money by sending the requested sum, along with a lamb that has a knife tied around its neck, by which he meant to signify his humility before the King and his willing recognition of the monarch's authority. Busto's unwritten communication in *La estrella* is, on the other hand, a forcefully expressed refutation of King Sancho's abuse of authority and a public exposure of his unlawful and unjust mode of ruling.

The hanged slave manifests the conflict between *honra* and *honor*, between the King and Busto, between *gusto* and *lo justo*, and between absence and presence. Earlier, when Don Arias had informed him of the preparations that had been made to facilitate his attempted seduction of Estrella, the King was very pleased and praised Natilde by proclaiming that "Castilla / estatuas la ha de labrar" (907-08). These words constitute an ironic anticipation of her fate: Busto literalizes the King's figurative language by converting her into a type of statue, one that publicly testifies neither to Natilde nor to the greatness of the King, but, rather, to the moral corruption of both. It is important to note in this context that Busto's unwritten communication is open and public, while nearly all of the King's communications are closed and secret. In assessing this situation, Brooks correctly observes that "Busto, by publicly executing Natilde for her part in allowing the king to enter his house, makes no effort to prevent possible gossip and, in fact, attracts attention to himself in the cause of pure justice" (12). This of course contradicts Brooks's own judgment (see above) that Busto does not care about public opinion; on the contrary, he *does* care about it and attempts, in fact, to utilize it to force the King to act with honor. The important point here is that Busto's openness and the King's secrecy together constitute an inversion of the modes by which king and subject conventionally operate, for Busto acts as a king ought to act, publicly and with honor, while King Sancho acts like a private citizen, that is, privately and guided by personal motives and desires.

When Busto reveals to Estrella that a stranger has illicitly entered the house, she vigorously defends her virtue:

> ¿En mi boca has visto
> palabras desenlazadas
> del honor con que las rijo?
> ¿Has visto alegres mis ojos
> de la cárcel de sus vidrios
> desatar rayos al aire,
> lisonjeros y lascivos?
> ¿En las manos de algún hombre
> viste algún papel escrito
> de la mía?
>
> (1281-90)

Rivers emphasizes that her writing a note of this type would constitute "an even greater threat to her modesty" ("Shame" 113); the written word is consistently portrayed in *La estrella* as a potentially subversive force.

When, in Act II, the King meets Sancho Ortiz for the first time, the scene is strikingly parallel to the first meeting between the King and Busto. Like Busto before him (278-88), Sancho ritually humbles himself before the monarch upon entering into his presence and insists on maintaining the proper social distance that is implicit in their relation as lord and vassal (1431-39). When the King tells him that there is a certain man that he wants executed secretly, Sancho actively argues against such secrecy:

Pues ¿cómo muerte en secreto
a un culpado se le da?
Poner su muerte en efeto
públicamente podrá
　　vuestra justicia, sin dalle
muerte en secreto; que así
vos os culpáis en culpalle,
pues dais a entender que aquí
sin culpa mandáis matalle.
　　Y dalle muerte, señor,
sin culpa, no es justa ley,
sino bárbaro rigor;
y un rey, sólo por ser rey,
se ha de respetar mejor.

(1478-91)

Sancho's words are true with a vengeance. The King can exercise "barbarous rigor" only because it is secret (no one else is to know about it) and because it is mediated (the King himself will not execute Busto: Sancho will enact it). According to Sancho, the very secrecy which the King proposes will make the execution suspect. Like Busto, Sancho explicitly emphasizes the importance of authorizing one's acts with a sense of full presence and moral responsibility, and the consequent necessity, especially in the case of a king, of acting openly and publicly.

The King is nonetheless able to convince Sancho to carry out the secret execution by telling him that the *culpado* had committed treason, and proceeds to present the two papers to Sancho. Harlan and Sara Sturm have astutely pointed out that the ambivalence of the word *papel* serves in this scene to emphasize Sancho's personal dilemma: "The dramatist . . . takes advantage of the double meaning associated with the word *papel*: Sancho el Bravo is, in effect, imposing on Sancho Ortiz a role consistent with the monarch's own distorted values but totally in opposition to the noble's sense of honor" ("The Two" 288). Sancho rejects the role that the King has assigned to him, that of secret and anonymous executioner. He cannot willingly "absent" himself in this way; he can only be himself, acting with full responsibility. He also rejects a *papel* in the literal sense, for he refuses to accept the King's written pardon, claiming that he trusts completely in his spoken promise:

> Estoy admirado
> de que tan poco conceto
>   tenga de mí Vuestra Alteza.
> ¡Yo cédula! ¡Yo papel!
> Tratadme con más llaneza,
> que más en vos que no en él
> confía aquí mi nobleza.
>   Si vuestras palabras cobran
> valor que los montes labra,
> y ellas cuanto dicen obran,
> dándome aquí la palabra,
> señor, los papeles sobran.
>   A la palabra remito
> la cédula que me dais,
> con que a vengaros me incito,
> porque donde vos estáis
> es excusado lo escrito.
>   Rompeldo, porque sin él
> la muerte le solicita
> mejor, señor, que con él;
> que en parte desacredita
> vuestra palabra el papel.
>   Sin papel, señor, aquí
> nos obligamos los dos,
> y prometemos así,
> yo de vengaros a vos
> y vos de librarme a mí.

(1555-81)

This is, without a doubt, the drama's most powerful indictment of written texts, as Rivers has noted ("Shame" 115). Sancho is shocked to see that the King could have so low an opinion of him as to offer him a written guarantee of freedom.

Sancho trusts much more in actual presence, the flesh-and-blood person, than he could in any mere piece of paper. This is doubly so in the case of a king, for he emphasizes the absolute authority of the King's spoken words by appealing to their institutionally performative nature ("cuanto dicen *obran*") that is dependent on a radical sense of presence:

> dándome *aquí* la palabra,
> señor, los papeles sobran
> . . . .
> . . . *donde vos estáis*
> es excusado lo escrito.

(When Don Arias later questions him in jail, Sancho emphasizes the utter seriousness with which the citizens of Seville
regard the literally performative nature of commissive speech
acts such as promises: "Decidle al Rey mi señor / que tienen
los sevillanos / las palabras en las manos . . ." [1845-47].)
According to Sancho, true honor lies in the consistency between
what one says ("palabras") and what one does ("manos"); thus
there is no need of a written guarantee, which would in fact
serve partially to discredit the oral promise. He therefore rips
up the King's pardon. It is an act that resonates with meaning
in reference to Natilde's *cédula*: this is the second time that a
promise of liberty, written by the hand of the King, has been
denied efficacy.

It is in the course of this conversation that the King suggests
to Sancho that he use the element of surprise to carry out the
execution: "Hallándole descuidado / puedes matarle" (1527-28).
As usual, the King chooses the mode of absence: he wants
Sancho to utilize a form of absence, or what amounts to hidden
presence (a surprise attack), in order to deceive Busto and
thereby kill him. If Busto is *descuidado*, he will not know that
he is being confronted and challenged; he will be far easier to
kill if he is unprepared to defend himself. But Sancho indignantly rejects this suggestion as being altogether inconsistent
with his own sense of personal integrity: "Cuerpo a cuerpo he
de matalle, / donde Sevilla lo vea, / en la plaza o en la calle"
(1532-34). Sancho insistently embodies the principle that honorable acts are performed in full presence and responsibility,
that is, "cuerpo a cuerpo." His moral position in this respect
clearly contrasts with and discredits that of the King.

Immediately following this exchange, Sancho receives a letter from Estrella, informing him of their imminent marriage
(1612-20). Unable to believe his good fortune, he needs to read
the letter twice in order to convince himself of its veracity
(1622-23; 1649-55). He then reads the King's order and finds
out that the "traitor" whom he must execute is none other than
Busto. As in the case of the letter from Estrella that has just
brought him such joy, Sancho again requires multiple readings
(1691-92; 1709-10; 1729-30) in order to digest its contents,
emotionally speaking.

The two written documents represent a torturous decision
that he must make, for they are inherently contradictory insofar

as Sancho himself is concerned. He realizes that killing Estrella's brother, in accordance with the King's written order and as he himself has promised, will eliminate any possibility of his marrying Estrella. In addition, the King's insistence upon secrecy in regard to Busto's execution has made Sancho suspect that this will be anything but an act of justice: ". . . aunque injusto el Rey, / debo obedecer su ley; / a él despúes Dios le castigue" (1752-54). Sancho, of course, finally keeps his promise to the King and kills Busto. He can do no other than embody the simple principle, invoked so tellingly by J. L. Austin in *How to Do Things with Words*, that ". . . our word is our bond" (10): his integrity and personal honor depend upon it. Much like Busto before him, in short, Sancho demonstrates a moral fortitude of which the King is obviously incapable.

The openly public execution of Busto, the man who was to be his brother-in-law, provokes Sancho's immediate imprisonment, and it is in prison that the famous "mad-scene" takes place.[8] During this hallucinatory scene, Sancho converses with a personification of Honor; this conversation is in reality a projection of the inner conflict that he is now facing. The dialogue between Sancho's divided self—ironically serving as a reflection of the King's own divided and warring self, despite the fact that the latter's situation is inspired by radically different motives—makes explicit that, in the modern world, *honra* is no longer a faithful indicator of *honor*. It points, rather, to the opposite of *honor*:

> —Honor, un necio y honrado
> viene a ser criado vuestro,
> por no exceder vuestras leyes.
> —Mal, amigo, lo habéis hecho,
> porque *el verdadero honor*
> *consiste ya en no tenerlo.*
> ¡A mí me buscáis allá,
> y ha mil siglos que estoy muerto!
> Dinero, amigo, buscad;
> que el honor es el dinero.
> ¿Qué hicisteis? —Quise cumplir
> una palabra. —Riendo
> me estoy: ¿palabras cumplís?
> Parecéisme majadero;

> que *es ya el no cumplir palabras*
> *bizarría en este tiempo.*
>
> (2478-93)

The concept of personal honor has, it seems, become an anachronism. It has been cynically perverted by a process of moral corruption that is exemplified by the King. Sancho remains faithful, nevertheless, to his own sense of personal honor and refuses to go back on his promise of secrecy to the King, even when questioned by the monarch himself, in prison:

> REY: ¿Quién te mandó darle muerte?
> SANCHO: Un papel.
> REY: ¿De quién?
> SANCHO: Si hablara
>   el papel, él lo dijera;
>   que es cosa evidente y clara;
>   mas los papeles rompidos
>   dan confusas las palabras.
>
> (2934-39)

Sancho reiterates his distrust of the written text: the only thing left of its producer is his or her traces—the written words—that cannot, in any case, be held accountable. Sancho implicitly denies the authority of the written word when he insists on describing its communicative power in terms of orality: "Si hablara / el papel, él lo dijera." He implies, with bitter irony, that even a written-upon piece of paper seems to have more of a sense of presence, integrity, and self-consistency than does this King, who—thus far—has not honorably lived up to his word by freeing him, as promised. Sancho, however, remains steadfast: he had accepted only the orally spoken words of the King as a promise of pardon and he will accept only his spoken words as the pardon itself.

The final written text in *La estrella* is Sancho's death sentence, issued by the city council, whose honor—like that of Sancho before them—is tested by the King's behavior, when he requests that Sancho be sentenced to exile. The fact that the monarch speaks *separately* to each of the local magistrates is consistent with his essential *modus operandi*. He approaches them in absence from one another and from all other witnesses

so as to continue to operate secretly; he wishes to spare
Sancho's life without publicly admitting his responsibility for
Busto's death. He hopes to influence privately the decision that
they will make in their public roles as upholders of the law. But
they are guided by their vision of public justice: they see
Sancho as guilty and sentence him accordingly, regardless of
the King's privately manifested desire. When the King reads
the sentence and demands to know why they did not comply
with his request, Don Pedro de Caus responds:

> Como a vasallos nos manda,
> mas como alcaldes mayores,
> no pidas injustas causas;
> que aquello es estar sin ellas,
> y aquesto es estar con varas,
> y el Cabildo de Sevilla
> es quien es.
>
> (2915-21)

Don Pedro makes a clear distinction between his status as a
private citizen (*vasallo*) and his public capacity in the role of
alcalde mayor, as symbolized by the wand of justice. His final
words are perhaps the strongest implied indictment of the
King's behavior throughout. Contrary to the King, who has
effectively absented himself from public responsibility by acting on personal whim and in a zone of secrecy, the council is
thoroughly present and integral, in all of the moral and public
senses those words have: "es quien es." This phrase clearly
echoes Sancho's earlier refusal of Don Arias's demand that he
reveal all that he knows about Busto's death:

> Yo soy quien soy,
> y siendo quien soy me venzo
> a mí mismo con callar,
> y a alguno que calla afrento . . .
> Quien es quien es, haga obrando
> como quien es; y con esto,
> de aquesta suerte los dos
> como quien somos haremos.
>
> (2340-47)

Sancho insists that essential presence is manifested by one's
own acts and that those acts—verbal and otherwise—actually

constitute the responsible, individual self. It is Sancho's and the council's honorable integrity, their utter sense of self in this regard, that forces the King to live up, finally, to his public responsibility. As McCrary has observed: "The city of Seville has demonstrated right procedure and strict adherence to the law as the only instrument capable of upholding justice and insuring the continuity of order" (511-12).

It is true that King Sancho has provided glimpses of repentance and even of an awakening sense of morality, prior to this moment. Indeed, McCrary's fine analysis of the play and his implied analogy between its structure and that of classical Greek tragedy emphasize the King's final confession and make the case that he has experienced a true ethical conversion (512-13). However, the still-strong influence of his counselor, Don Arias, shows that the King's progress has perhaps not been so great as McCrary implies. From the beginning, he follows his own *gusto* with the consistent encouragement, advice, and aid of Don Arias. Indeed, the counselor serves functionally to make of the monarch's absence a double absence, for the King himself never seems to act or even to make any decision without the counsel of his *privado*. It is Don Arias who advises the King to favor Busto in order to accomplish the seduction of Estrella; it is Don Arias who initiates illicit contact with Natilde and promises her liberty in the name of the King; it is Don Arias who presses for Busto's execution; and it is Don Arias who suggests Sancho Ortiz as the man to carry it out.

The King's final public admission that he was behind Busto's death may be considered his first truly responsible act—his first completely public and oral utterance as a king. But it is not an independent one, for he does not utter a single word until he sees that there is no way of escaping this public admission other than by allowing Sancho Ortiz to die. In desperation, therefore, he turns to his counselor and asks what he should do (2966-68). Don Arias's one-word response, "Hablad," shows that his control over the King continues until the very end of the drama, that is, that no true conversion has taken place. The one term that should most indicate the King's public presence and responsibility—by way of an emphatic orality ("Hablad")—ironically serves here to manifest his continuing ethical absence.

Interestingly, most of the King's oral communication throughout *La estrella* partakes of absence, that is, the absence of any third-party witnesses. His conversations are, for the most part, private and one-to-one; he tends to speak to individuals, not to groups. The King talks individually, for example, to the *alcaldes* near the end of the drama and most often speaks secretly to Don Arias in asides that serve functionally to exclude all others. But the citizens of Seville, by their own honorable sense of duty, force him to speak publicly, in all the senses of that term.

The drama ends, therefore, on a rather ambiguous note. Whatever lesson has been learned by the King has proved enormously costly in human terms: the life of an honorable man, Busto Tavera, and the love of two exemplary people, Sancho Ortiz and Estrella. These two go their separate ways and the moral fate of the King (and, by extension, of the entire realm) is left open. We do not know, at the end of *La estrella*, if the King's public admission of responsibility represents a lasting social order or if we have simply witnessed a postponing of the moral and social chaos that is one of the constitutive signs of tragedy. Clearly, the actual history of King Sancho IV (his rebellion against his father, Alfonso X, and the ensuing chaos that characterized his reign) was well known to Golden Age audiences and appears to point in the direction of the latter.

To summarize: King Sancho in *La estrella de Sevilla* is the producer of various written texts throughout, and it is by way of writing that he can give orders *in absentia*. The play thereby dramatizes the tragic consequences of a moral absence that undercuts the code of personal honor. We may see now, in retrospect, that the drama's written texts are organized in pairs whose members contradict one another. The two petitions presented to the King at the beginning of Act I contradict one another in that they are mutually exclusive: the monarch can award the military post to only one of the two *pretendientes*. The *cédula* with which the King bribes Natilde in Act II is the secret contradiction of those "escrituras / tan firmes y seguras" (556-57) that ostensibly guarantee Estrella's honorable wedding to Sancho Ortiz. Finally, the King's written order to kill Busto Tavera is contradictory to the letter that Sancho receives soon after from Estrella, announcing to him their imminent marriage: Sancho's carrying out of the first will make the second an impossibility.

By portraying written texts in this way, that is, as mutually contradictory, *La estrella* reveals how their fragile authority is ultimately derived from and dependent upon that which inheres in those "authentic oral performative utterance[s]" of which they are mere inscribed "reminders" (Rivers, "Shame" 115). The only written text in the drama that is not paired up with its own written contradiction is Sancho's death sentence. *Its* contradiction is the King's final and fully performative oral admission of responsibility. This is intelligible in terms of the dichotomy of writing and speaking that is established throughout: the King's pattern of absential subversion, effected largely by way of written documents, can be stopped only by the presence that is implicit in oral communication. *La estrella de Sevilla* dramatizes the age-old conflict between personal desire and public duty. It manifests this conflict by way of an ideology that champions the metaphysics of presence, that is, in the opposition between written and oral communication, an opposition that is resolved only when the King is forced, finally, to speak truthfully and publicly as a king.

La estrella remains an elusive and suggestive drama, in spite of efforts to examine it according to the various oppositions described throughout this chapter. Despite the seeming clarity of such oppositions as self/other, presence/absence, desire/justice, writing/orality, private/public, and *honra/honor*, the drama problematizes all of them by showing that these terms are not independent or absolute, but rather mutually defining and dependent. (One clear example of this has been discussed above: both Sancho Ortiz and Busto, despite their inclination toward personal *honor* that is based upon morality, *do* care about social *honra*. Even that seeming ideological absolute, *honor* based upon *presence*, is shown to be yet one more form of cultural—if not literal—inscription.) At the center of *La estrella* is thus a radical questioning of the terms that define and delimit society itself: institutions such as honor and justice. Even the *self*, posited metaphysically as a given and unitary essence, becomes part of the dialectic, a process rather than a product. *La estrella* continues to fascinate us because of this essential duality—because it looks back nostalgically at a lost metaphysics while at the same time acknowledging that *différance* has irremediably invaded the world.

"Seeing and Not Seeing"

Interpretation and Drift in Mira de Amescua's
El ejemplo mayor de la desdicha

Antonio Mira de Amescua's *El ejemplo mayor de la desdicha*
(1625?) has received almost no critical attention, despite the
fact that it is a fine example of a subgenre of Spanish Golden
Age drama: the *dramas de privanza*. These dramas form a
discrete body of plays that, as Raymond R. MacCurdy has
stated in his valuable and perceptive study of this category of
comedias, "dramatize the rise and fall of royal ministers and
favorites" (11). They have long been regarded as having an
essentially didactic function, that of demonstrating the inconstancy of human endeavor and of Fate, relative to the eternal
and unchanging nature of the Divine Will. One of the characteristics of this genre is therefore the recurring image of the
wheel of Fortune. These dramas have also been related to an
abiding popular interest in exploring and defining the social
status of the *privado*.

The action begins with the homecoming of Belisario, the drama's protagonist, from war in Persia. Teodora, a lady of the
court who was once rejected by Belisario because of his love
for Antonia, another lady of the court, has since married
the Emperor Justinian and is now seeking revenge against the
returning hero. She has secretly ordered Leoncio, a military
commander recently dismissed from court, to kill him. Disguised as a poor soldier returning from war, Leoncio begs
Belisario for alms, claiming that he had fought under the well-
known commander, Leoncio. Belisario responds generously,
declares that Leoncio was unjustly dismissed from court, and
promises to help put the commander back in the Emperor's
good graces. In response to this kindness, Leoncio renounces
the murder attempt, reveals who he is, and tells Belisario that a
certain woman, whose identity he refuses to divulge, is seeking

to kill him. This interchange sets the pattern for the entire drama: Teodora, seeing that her first attempt has failed, engages first Narses and then Filipo—both courtiers—to kill Belisario, whom Justinian has now elevated to the position of *privado*. Like Leoncio before them, however, they are literally disarmed by the protagonist's kindness and virtue. Teodora finally attempts to murder Belisario herself, but is prevented by her husband Justinian, who catches her in the act. When the Emperor orders Teodora to be sent away from court and Belisario intercedes on her behalf, her wrath toward the protagonist is converted to love. However, her love changes back to hatred when Belisario once again rejects her. Teodora manages to convince Justinian that Belisario has betrayed him by making sexual advances upon her. She thereby succeeds in reversing the pattern whereby Belisario's enemies are transformed into friends and, invoking the sensitive area of male honor, transforms his most powerful protector, Justinian, into his most dangerous enemy. The Emperor orders Belisario's office and riches stripped from him, imprisons him, and then orders his eyes to be gouged out. Belisario's fall from power ends in solitude, poverty, blindness, and death. In the final (and rather anticlimactic) scene, Antonia reveals Teodora's treachery to Justinian. The Emperor repudiates his wife and offers to make up for his unjust treatment of Belisario by marrying Antonia. She refuses.

El ejemplo begins with a description of Belisario's homecoming by Floro, the play's *gracioso*:

> Como tus hechos divinos
> son *asombro* de la muerte,
> todos han salido a *verte*.
> Ciudades son los caminos.
>   Los riscos y árboles son
> *miradores*, donde están
> pasmados hombres, que dan
> *ojos* a la *admiración*.
>   En el vulgo incierto y vario
> cada cual está diciendo:
> "¡Válgame Dios, que estoy *viendo*
> al valiente Belisario!"
>
> (1-12)

Floro's description contains several terms that are related, often etymologically, to visual perception: *asombro* (related to *sombra*), *ver*, *miradores*, *ojos*, *admiración* (related to *mirar*) and *viendo*. This is the beginning of a series of references to visual perception that is developed consistently throughout the entire drama. Indeed, MacCurdy is quite correct when he asserts that "the theme of 'seeing and not seeing' is fundamental to the meaning of *El ejemplo mayor de la desdicha*" (163).

Floro says that Belisario is the *admiración* of men. The term *admiración*, much like *asombro*, is ambivalent, for it is used to refer to the sense of wonder or surprise inspired by extremity of whatever nature, either positive or negative. It is precisely this inherent reversibility of the term *admirar* that *El ejemplo* exploits: by the end of the drama, Belisario is—as a tragic figure—most worthy of *admiración*, but in a spirit very much opposed to that in which Floro appears to be describing him here. *Admiratio* is, of course, one of the constituent elements of tragedy as it is defined by Aristotle in the *Poetics* (109).[1] The drama's opening lines thus serve to foreshadow the enacting of *admiratio*'s potential reversibility while at the same time emphasizing the motif of perception.

The term *admiración* is repeatedly associated with Belisario. In Act II, for example, Justinian refers to him in the most praiseworthy terms as "admiración de los hombres" (1646) and later recounts that several kings, inspired by his exploits, had once come to see the warrior in person:

> Cuatro reyes, *admirados*
> de su fama, hasta mi corte
> por verle peregrinaron;
> y estando en presencia suya
> en un éxtasis y pasmo
> de *admiración* se quedaban
> atentos y embelesados.
>
> (1785-91)

Near the end of the drama, Belisario himself is patently aware of the *admiración* that his own fall from power will inspire:

> (Casi llego a desear
> la adversidad que estoy viendo,
> porque pienso ser cayendo
> el varón más singular;
> porque el subir y el medrar
> son escalas de la vida,

67

> y honra en mí tan merecida,
> pues en la virtud se alcanza,
> no *admirará* mi privanza
> y *admirará* mi caída).
>
> (2328-37)

His climb to power should not surprise others: such honors are the conventional rewards of virtue, which Belisario attempts to practice throughout. What will inspire *admiración* is the fact that he has fallen *in spite of* his virtue and that Fate is, in effect, blindly indifferent to human endeavor and morality.

The word *mirar* also appears frequently throughout. Near the end of the drama, for example, Justinian has difficulty confronting his own final punishment of Belisario: "¿Este espectáculo *miran* / mis ojos?" (2725-26). In the drama's final scene, Antonia refuses the Emperor's offer of marriage, for she has learned something of the inconstancy of Fate by considering the example of Belisario, whose unjust treatment at the hands of the Emperor gives her a very good sense of just what sort of fate she herself might expect: "*Miro* ejemplos" (2819). These variations on *mirar* and *admirar* are an aspect of the motif of perception that is prevalent throughout. In effect, the principal characters are made to suffer because of the limits of perception: they are inevitably deceived by appearances. The character who most exploits human fallibility in this regard is Teodora.

In Act I, for example, Teodora forces Antonia to act contrary to her desires and to reject Belisario. Teodora threatens Antonia by telling her that if she should show favor in any way to Belisario, harm will come to him:

> No he de castigar *sus* yerros
> en tí sino en él, y ansí
> tu amor será su veneno.
> Tú le matas si le quieres . . .
> (562-65; emphasis in original)

The specifically communicative irony of this situation is that Teodora has subverted the conventional code of signification and created a new one that endows signs with meanings that are the opposite of their original ones. In order to safeguard Belisario's well-being, Antonia knows that she must—

paradoxically—reject him, as long as they are both in the presence of Teodora:

> Mi pecho amando es ingrato,
> favoreciéndole es fiero,
> si le aborrezco le quiero,
> y si le quiero le mato;
> su vida está en mi recato,
> su muerte está en mi favor. . . .

(667-72)

Teodora succeeds in subverting communication between Antonia and Belisario, for the protagonist does not know that the conventional code has been inverted in this way and he is thereby deceived. As if to emphasize the question of perception and appearances, this scene revolves around "seeing and not seeing," that is, the ways in which eye contact is or is not established:

BELISARIO: Déme vuestra majestad
la mano.
TEODORA: —Disimulemos,
ira y venganza.—Seáis
bienvenido. Alza[d].—Yo vuelvo
a *ver* si Antonia le *mira*.—
(Aparte, a Antonia.) *Baja esos ojos* al suelo,
que le costará la vida.
ANTONIA: Muero por *mirar*le, y temo
desta tigre los enojos.
¡Remedio, cielos, remedio!
BELISARIO: ¡Ay, Antonia de mi vida!
Gracias al amor, que *veo*
el cielo de tu hermosura.
Dudoso del bien que tengo
no doy crédito a los *ojos*.
Mas ¡ay de mí!, ¿qué es aquesto?
Los suyos no ha levantado
para mirarme. Recelo . . .
Mas, ¿qué recelo, qué digo,
si con mis dudas la ofendo,
con mis sospechas la agravio?
Recato ha sido discreto.
Ella su amor disimula.
ANTONIA: Mas os valiera estar *ciegos*,

69

> *ojos*, si no habéis de *ver*
> lo que con el alma quiero.

(585-610)

Teodora creates a visual and communicative disjunction between the two lovers. Near the end of the passage, Belisario
notes that Antonia has averted her eyes, but incorrectly ascribes
this to her sense of discretion rather than to her true motive,
which is to spare him from harm.

Upon his second return from war, this time in Africa, Belisario
approaches the royal palace, where he sees two men attacking
a lone one. He reads the situation *conventionally*: seeing an
unfair fight, he goes to the aid of the lone man against his cow-
ardly attackers. Ironically, the man whom he defends and
whose life he saves—Filipo—was actually on the way to kill
him. Unknowingly, Belisario defends Filipo against two others,
Leoncio and Narses, who are risking their lives to protect him
from the very man he is rescuing (1200-10). This situation
comes about in part because the darkness of the evening prevents Belisario from identifying all of these men. This darkness
is a literalization of a more general darkness that pervades the
entire play and that connotes the ultimate ambivalence and
reversibility of all appearances. The play's insistent use of
visual imagery and darkness underscores the motif of deception and the unreliability of appearances.

When Justinian praises the sleeping Belisario, he implicitly
emphasizes the *privado*'s perceptual limitations when he refers
specifically to his "dormidos . . . ojos" (1634-35). These sleeping eyes are in contrast to those invoked in the Emperor's later
promise of constant vigil over Belisario, a promise that is likewise framed in terms of his own figurative ability to see, like
the mythological giant, with a hundred eyes: "*Yo te serviré de
Argos*" (1675; emphasis in original). This vow is rendered
ironic and roundly contradicted by the punishment that Justinian
ultimately inflicts upon his *privado* near the end of the drama,
a punishment that is explicitly visual, as well: "Los ojos han de
pagar / lo que pecaron los ojos" (2312-13). Belisario's putative
crime, that of "putting his eyes" upon Teodora, will be punished
by means of those same eyes.

It is by way of his rise and fall, however, that Belisario
finally learns to see in a more figurative and profound sense,

as when he meditates, in Act III, on the mutability of all human affairs:

> Si es mortal
> cualquiera por más que prive,
> ¿qué merced eterna vive?
> Todas mueren, claro está,
> porque es hombre quien las da
> y es hombre quien las recibe.
> Todo favor es violento
> cuando no viene de Dios.
>
> (2342-49)

According to Belisario, all mortal favor is "violent," that is, mutable and unstable; only God's favor is reliable. Implied by this statement is, of course, the literal violence that appears to be the result of courtly power. Filipo has already commented upon the mutability and violence of courtly intrigue:

> Desde César, el imperio
> todo es tragedias y muertes
> de varones principales.
> Por invidia o por venganza,
> teatros son de la mudanza
> los palacios imperiales.
>
> (1148-53)

The final definition of the term *violento* in *Autoridades* is particularly applicable to this context: "Se aplica también a lo que se executa contra el modo regular, u fuera de la razón, y justicia." Belisario now perceives that God alone, not emperors, acts with absolute justice. He also comes to a full awareness of the ambiguity of appearances:

> Entre las cosas más claras
> ojos engañados vimos;
> los remos parecen corbos
> en las ondas y zafiros
> del mar, y paloma negra
> suele volar, y, a los visos
> del sol, parecer sus alas
> oro y púrpura de Tiro.
> Pues si en el agua y el sol
> vemos engaños, rey mío,

71

¡en las lenguas de los hombres
cuantas veces se habrán visto!

(2526-37)

Belisario uses specifically visual imagery to emphasize the utter deceptiveness of appearances and thereby hopes to convince the Emperor of the falsity of Teodora's accusation.

The gouging out of Belisario's eyes and his resulting blindness are the final literalization, on the level of the action, of what has been, in effect, a running symbolic motif.[2] His literal blindness, much like Oedipus's, connotes a higher, more figurative seeing, that consists—paradoxically—of an awareness of the essential darkness and ambivalence of the human condition. The significant difference between Oedipus's blindness and Belisario's is that, whereas Oedipus's is self-inflicted and brought about by causes that are within himself and that he finally recognizes, Belisario's is inflicted upon him by forces that he but dimly perceives and that are very much out of his control. Belisario has learned the arbitrariness, the very "blindness" of Fate that is brought to bear by Teodora and Justinian and that more broadly manifests itself by way of the ceaselessly transitory human condition. Near the end of the drama, Belisario asks: "¿En qué han pecado los ojos / que la luz vital les quitan?" (2654-55). It is this final unanswerable question that sums up the irony and pathos of Belisario's rise and fall.

Inscribed texts are one of the chief manifestations of the darkness that pervades *El ejemplo*. Like Belisario's final blindness, various forms of writing and inscription are the specific literalization—on the level of the drama's action—of a more general concept: the "text" of Fate that is illegible to all but its Author. It is precisely Fate's seeming arbitrariness, its inherent "illegibility," that constitutes much of the drama's darkness.

The first example of actual inscriptions found in *El ejemplo* are two rings on which the Emperor has had the royal seal inscribed. When Belisario returns from war at the beginning of the drama, Justinian gives him one of them:

Dos *anillos* con dos sellos
mandé hacer de un propio modo,
porque podamos en todo
ser los dos uno con ellos.
Toma el uno, y la amistad

finezas haga y extremos.
Cástor y Pollux seremos.
Belisario es mi mitad.
         (361-68; emphasis in original)

The Emperor's act is something of a paradox, for it constitutes—on different levels—both a fusion and a division. By
giving Belisario a ring that is identical to his own, Justinian
figuratively joins himself to Belisario with words that are
strangely reminiscent of a marriage vow: "podamos en todo /
ser los dos uno con ellos." This "union" shows the depth of
Justinian's feeling for his court favorite, but because the ring
contains the royal seal, it also has serious civic implications,
for it makes Belisario the symbolic, if not the functional, equal
of the Emperor. With the royal seal, the *privado* can theoretically give orders and carry out official affairs; he may even
potentially serve as a type of surrogate emperor in the absence
of the monarch himself. This is a serious breach of protocol on
the part of Justinian; the rings represent a transgressing of
institutional norms, for they constitute an unprecedented, if
symbolic, division of power.

Inscription is normally what allows for the institutional
division and diffusion of authority. In the form of official seals
and documents, it enables a government to function institutionally outside of the physical presence of the ruler. Like the
King's letters in *El villano en su rincón*, the royal seal constitutes a diffusion of power, a token of the *official* presence of
government. In the case of the ring, however, this diffusion is
radical to the point of subversion: the absolute uniqueness of
the royal seal, that which explicitly connects it to royal preroga-
tive, has been symbolically undermined by Justinian's act. The
Emperor's figurative marriage to his *privado* undercuts his
civic role as ruler as well as his marriage to Teodora. Indeed,
Justinian's publicly professed support of Belisario, along with
his claim that the *privado* is worth more to him than anyone or
anything (1070-89), is precisely what rekindles Teodora's
hatred and helps to bring about the *privado*'s ultimate downfall. Such are the dangers of *privanza* and the division of power,
the beginning of which is signaled by these rings.

In contrast to this ring—that indirectly helps to bring about
Belisario's ultimate downfall—another ring later helps to save

his life. When Belisario aids Filipo in fighting off his two attackers, the latter gives him a ring out of gratitude; when Filipo later recognizes it as the one he had given his unidentified savior, he is converted from Belisario's would-be assassin to his friend. The beginning of Belisario's fall from power is signaled when this same Filipo comes to relieve him of the original ring with the royal seal upon it (2338-42). In effect, once Justinian is led by Teodora to believe that the honor of his marriage to her has been violated, he immediately "divorces" himself from Belisario by taking his ring back. Thus it is that the ring takes on a form of textuality all its own, by marking and symbolizing—in very precise terms—Belisario's rise to and fall from power.

Another form of inscription appears just after the Emperor prevents Teodora from doing away with his *privado*. As though trying to make explicit to Teodora what Belisario means to him, Justinian orders coins engraved that bear his image on one side and Belisario's on the other:

> Batan moneda, que a un lado
> tenga mi rostro y en otro
> el de Belisario orlado
> de letras que digan: "Este
> sustenta el imperio sacro."
>
> (1835-39)

These coins represent a continuation of the same structure associated with the rings: a symbolic division of civic power, in the name of personal friendship. This structure appears again when Justinian declares Belisario to be his successor (1843-44) and proceeds literally to divide the other symbols of royal power, by giving him half of the imperial staff (1846-48) and half of the crown (1850-54). Justinian's dividing of institutional symbols that are conventionally unique and indivisible constitutes a form of public subversion that is the counterpart of Teodora's private one. These material symbols of power (rings, coins, staff, and crown), all forms of cultural inscription in themselves, constitute a metatext: a literalization, on the level of the action, of the motif of divided power. This scene constitutes a clear contrast to the final one of *El villano en su rincón*, in which the unitary material symbols of royalty represent a consolidation—rather than a division—of power.

Letters are another form of inscription that is found in *El ejemplo*. Near the beginning of the drama, Floro uses a letter as part of a trick to gain the Emperor's favor: one of the returning soldiers, Fabricio, is carrying a testimonial to his bravery in battle, written by his commander. Floro manages to steal it from Fabricio when the latter's attention is diverted and substitutes for it a blank piece of paper:

> Si desta caja pudiera
> sacarle un papel sería
> buena fortuna la mía,
> por que servirme pudiera;
>   que él mismo me lo ha mostrado:
> ni nombre ni señas tray.

Sácale un papel de una caja de latón y métele otro [en blanco].

> Valientes industrias hay
> para un gallina soldado.
>   Topélo; el alcance sigo.
> ¡Helo! En esto no soy manco.
> Zámpole un papel en blanco,
> que acaso traigo conmigo.
> (389-400)

Floro presents the stolen paper to the Emperor, thereby "proving" that he has served bravely as a soldier and is worthy of reward, as he had earlier stated to Belisario (18-19; 237-38). The Emperor proceeds to read the written testimony out loud:

> "Gran señor, el que ésta lleva
> es un valiente soldado.
> Dos banderas ha ganado.
> No hay hombre que a más se atreva.
> *Julio, maestre de campo*."
> (421-25; emphasis in original)

The final line of Julio's inscribed statement is ironically true in reference to Floro, for there *is* no "hombre que a más se atreva," as his illicit and brazen act so plainly shows. Justinian rewards Floro, based upon the words of the written testimony (429-31).

This example of writing demonstrates what Derrida has identified as its essential *drift*: its ability to be recontextualized renders unreachable its original intentions and therefore subject to theoretically infinite reinterpretation (see Introduction, pp. 6-7). In this case, the man identified by Julio's written words is simply "el que ésta lleva," not a specifically named individual: the testimony is, therefore, doubly subject to drift. It is a text that by its utilization of a pronominal shifter (*ésta*) depends, like the spoken word, upon the oral/aural context for its meaning. It is a writing that depends, paradoxically, on immediate *presence* for its referential value. Floro, of course, uses this to his own advantage and deceives the Emperor by validating the letter with his own presence.

Floro's deception, however, also depends radically upon *absence* in several ways. He obviously depends on the absence of the author of the written testimonial, Julio, in order to appropriate it and thereby authorize his own claims of bravery at war. He also utilizes absence by functionally displacing the true owner of the paper, putting himself in his stead, and thereby receiving rewards that were meant for someone else. Interestingly, *this* absence was anticipated by another: Floro takes advantage of Fabricio's absence within the immediate oral context. He notices that Fabricio's attention is diverted by the Emperor: "Mirando al Emperador / *Fabricio quedó elevado*" (387-88; emphasis in original). It is Fabricio's being *elevado* ("transported," "absent") that enables Floro to steal the paper and thus to pull off the deception in the first place.

Of course, when Fabricio sees how handsomely the Emperor has rewarded Floro, a man he knows to be a scoundrel, he proceeds to present Justinian with what he believes is *his* written testimony:

> FABRICIO: Yo soy, señor, un soldado
> pobre, que en Persia serví,
> según en éste verás.
>
> Dale otro papel [en blanco].
>
> EMPERADOR: No has servido; servirás,
> que el papel lo dice así.
> Si en blanco tráis los servicios,
> en blanco quedarte puedes.
>
> (440-46)

When the Emperor sees the blank sheet, he concludes that Fabricio simply did not serve at all. He therefore rips it up and gives him nothing. Floro's deception emphasizes the Emperor's all-too-human limitations; like Belisario, Justinian is deceived by appearances. In this case, Floro's subversive and selfish recontextualization of the letter does not have any serious or permanent effects. The trick—perpetrated by an exploitation of *absence*—is discovered and ultimately remedied by the *presence* of Julio, the letter's writer, who appears near the end of the drama. He clears up the situation by identifying the true Fabricio in front of the Emperor and forcing Floro to give up the reward that he had illicitly received (2584-609). Julio's letter is an anticipation of another letter that appears near the beginning of Act III and that, like Julio's, is subject to a radical recontextualization that proves equally successful in deceiving Justinian. In contrast to Julio's letter, however, this later one has permanent and devastating effects, as we shall see.

Written texts appear once again in the form of the petitions that the Emperor hands over to his *privado* and that represent the familiar motif of the division of power: Justinian delegates to Belisario the decision of who is to govern Italy. Belisario allows Fate to make the decision by merely shuffling the petitions; he signs the one that comes out on top (Narses's) to indicate his choice and promptly falls asleep. As it turns out, this same Narses happens to be on his way to carry out Belisario's execution, as per Teodora's orders. When Narses enters Belisario's chamber, he sees that the *privado* has chosen him to govern Italy; he promptly renounces the murder plot and leaves, but not without inscribing a warning on the petition that a certain unnamed woman is attempting to kill Belisario. When the *privado* awakens and reads the anonymous warning, he interprets it as referring to Antonia:

> . . . ¿Tan tirano
> es el corazón de Antonia?
> ¿Tan apriesa está buscando
> mi muerte?
>
> (896-99)

He does so because he was deceived by Antonia's earlier indifference to him, which, we remember, had been secretly imposed upon her by Teodora.

The petition ends up in the hands of the Emperor, who, when he reads it, learns of the threat to Belisario's life and that an unidentified woman is behind it (990-97). In order to discover her identity, Justinian confronts Narses with the petition and asks if he recognizes the handwriting of the message that is scrawled upon it (1256). Narses admits that it is his, but refuses to reveal to the Emperor the identity of the woman who was plotting Belisario's death. His refusal to do so is, however, as good as a direct accusation, as Justinian confirms in an aside: "Quien es me ha dicho ya; que si no fuera / Teodora, claro está que lo dijera" (1268-69).

This interchange is similar to one that occurs soon after between Belisario and Filipo. The latter, while admitting his involvement in a plot to kill Belisario, is nevertheless unwilling to reveal explicitly who is behind it:

> BELISARIO: ¿Quién es?
> FILIPO: Decillo quisiera
> aunque mi palabra ofendo,
> pero vé tu discurriendo.
> BELISARIO: ¿Es Camila?
> FILIPO: No es tan fiera.
> BELISARIO: ¿Marcia?
> FILIPO: Piadosa es también.
> BELISARIO: ¿Antonia?
> FILIPO: No lo intentó.
> BELISARIO: Dime si es Antonia.
> FILIPO: No.
> BELISARIO: Hágante los Cielos bien.
>   ¿Es Teodora?
> FILIPO: Adiós, amigo.
> BELISARIO: ¿Vas callando?
> FILIPO: Hablando voy.
> BELISARIO: ¿Tú eres mi amigo?
> FILIPO: Sí soy.
> BELISARIO: Dilo, pues.
> FILIPO: Ya te lo digo.
>
>   (1580-91)

Filipo *does* reveal that Teodora is behind the murder plot, but only indirectly, that is, by way of implication. He will not explicitly say so. Teodora is "unnameable" in this and in the previous example. She is referred to only in secret and indirect ways: when Belisario dares to say her name, Filipo signals his own imminent exit and absence ("Adiós, amigo") from the scene and allows silence itself to name Teodora. This is most appropriate, for, as a consistent disruptor of communicative contexts, she is the embodiment of the darkness and incomprehensibility that animate *El ejemplo.*

At the end of Act I, Justinian reads some letters that inform him that war has broken out in Africa and that he must send Belisario to fight. The letters presage the absence of the protagonist from the court, but the very act of reading on the part of the Emperor intermittently "absents" *him* from the immediate oral context. This enables another secret and fragmentary dialogue between Belisario and Antonia to take place simultaneously, as the stage directions inform us:

> Vase cada uno por su puerta, y adviértese que el EMPERADOR está en medio leyendo, y un criado alumbrando, y BELISARIO habla a hurto con ANTONIA, llegándose, y desviándose cuando llama el EMPERADOR, y ella se está siempre en la puerta por que no la vea el EMPERADOR. (p. 192)

This dialogue is, however, conditioned and contextualized by earlier acts of communication that, imposed by Teodora, have caused Belisario's misconstruing of the facts. He therefore mistakenly accuses Antonia of having twice attempted to murder him. It is with this scene—the very image of disjunction, misunderstanding, and fragmented presence—that Act I ends.

Another letter appears near the beginning of Act III: a love note from Belisario to Antonia (2112). Communication between the two lovers is just as indirect and secret at this juncture as it was at the end of Act I, but in this case Teodora is present and, spotting the note from Belisario hidden in Antonia's sleeve, becomes aware of the hidden act of communication that is about to take place. She proceeds to interrupt it by demanding that Antonia give the note to her. The intercepted note is, obviously, a communication that fails in the sense that its intended recipient, Antonia, never reads it. Like the letter that Floro steals at the beginning of the drama, this one emphasizes the potential drift of all written communication and the risks that it entails. Teodora's interception and subsequent recontextualization of the note will enable her to take

vengeance upon Belisario, for she can now cast her earlier attempted murder of the *privado* in a new light that will divert
all of the blame from herself to Belisario. She proceeds to justify her earlier act of violence against the *privado* by telling
Justinian that Belisario had attempted to seduce her:

> ... rica de tu favor,
> con soberbia y vanidad,
> hallarás que la amistad
> intenta tu deshonor.
>
> (2202-05)

This fiction is most ironic, for it succeeds in reversing and
thereby masking what had actually occurred, namely, Teodora's
attempted seduction of Belisario. The Empress's blatant mis-
representation of her own past treachery anticipates her recontextualization of the note she has intercepted.

Immediately following her accusation, she "faints," thereby
absenting herself from the immediate oral/aural context. As
usual, Teodora is a cipher of absence: much like King Sancho in
La estrella de Sevilla, she invariably functions in an insidious
and indirect way. Having established a new context for interpretation on the part of her husband, she can let the note do
her speaking for her, as Justinian himself observes when he
finds it:

> Sin duda, en este papel
> me escribe la triste suma
> de rigores alevosos,
> porque a labios vergonzosos
> sirve de lengua la pluma.
>
> (2217-21)

The Emperor at first mistakenly assumes that Teodora has
written the note out of a sense of shame. He proceeds to read
the note:

> ... "Cuando pensé que querías
> matarme, sin ofenderte,
> estimaba aquella muerte
> más que las victorias mías.
> Porque morir a tus manos

fuera vivir mereciendo,
como agora estoy muriendo,
a tus ojos soberanos."

(2226-33)

Although Justinian is able to identify the author (he recognizes Belisario's handwriting), he has no clue as to its intended addressee and is forced to conjecture in terms of the immediate context, which is masterfully provided by Teodora. He immediately jumps to the conclusion that Teodora was the note's intended recipient: "Bien se vé que estas razones / sólo son para Teodora" (2236-37). He proceeds to interpret Teodora's fainting as part of that context: a sign of the depth of her feeling and love for him, and of her stained sense of honor (2242-45). Justinian reaches conclusions that are mistaken but natural, given the context that Teodora has provided. Indeed, he cannot interpret otherwise, unaware as he is that the note was intended for Antonia and that it refers to earlier misimpressions held by Belisario.

By exploiting this particular written text's drift, made more radical by its lack of a signature or an addressee, and by giving it a new and fictive context, Teodora directs Justinian's reading and interpretation. Like Floro's deception of the Emperor at the beginning of the drama, hers is successful, for Justinian's love of Belisario has now been turned to anger: "Su pensamiento villano / este papel manifiesta" (2284-85). But Teodora's method is the reverse of Floro's: whereas the *gracioso* had lent authority to the written words of Julio's note with his own *presence* (the words that he speaks), Teodora lends authority to the words that she speaks with a written text and by making herself *absent*.

Teodora's illicit utilization of this written note brings about the drama's *peripecia*: the beginning of the *privado*'s fall from grace. Belisario's fall not only begins but also ends with a written text—the order effecting final punishment for his apparent crime:

"Sacaréis con cien soldados de guarda a Belisario, fuera de los muros; y allí le saquen los ojos, pues con ellos ofendió la cesárea majestad poniéndolos en lo sagrado de su honor; y ninguno le socorra, pena de mi desgracia, porque quiero que mendigue quien usó mal de las riquezas que tenía. *Justiniano, Emperador.*" (p. 272; emphasis in original)

Contrary to other written documents in *El ejemplo*, this one is signed and personally delivered to its intended recipients— Leoncio and Filipo—by its author. It leaves little room for recontextualization or interpretation. It has much of the imme- diacy of a spoken communication and is, consequently, not subject to the potential drift that has so radically influenced the other written documents in this drama. One irony of this situa- tion is that so firm and fixed a text is the direct result of a tragic misunderstanding of reality on the part of Justinian, who, as Emperor, gives it all the absolute authority and weight of officialdom.

The other irony of this punishment is the apparent injustice with which Belisario is repaid for attempting to act virtuously. By the end of the drama, he is reduced to begging for alms from those whom he has most helped, such as Narses, Filipo, and Leoncio, who must now refuse him any such reciprocal kind- ness precisely because of the Emperor's written order. The same injustice may be invoked in reference to the Emperor him- self: aside from having saved Justinian's life various times in battle (2404-63), Belisario has greatly aided and increased the empire by his military exploits (2464-95). There is great irony, therefore, in the Emperor's unjust treatment of Belisario and, by implication, in the legendary aura that surrounds the histori- cal figure of Justinian as codifier of the ancient laws of Rome and dispenser of its justice. Soon after preventing Teodora from killing Belisario, Justinian maintains that he must live up to his name and administer justice, regardless of his personal relation to whoever might be behind this attempted act of treachery:

> Mas si el derecho civil
> y leyes de los romanos
> pongo en orden y reduzgo
> a un volumen reformado,
> justiciero debo ser,
> satisfacer debo agravios,
> castigar debo delitos[,]
> y huir respetos humanos.
>
> (1808-15)

In light of the justice that Justinian *does* administer in punishing Belisario, these words are tragically hollow: so much for the efficacy of justice that has been textually codified and inscribed.

Aside from those written documents described thus far, there is one other that merits some attention. It appears in Act II and serves as a fitting emblem for much of the play-acting, pretense, and deception that occurs throughout. We have seen, for example, that Floro early on pretends that he fought bravely at war, in order to reap the benefits earned by another; Leoncio, disguised as a poor soldier, refers to himself in the third person and pretends that he had fought under his own command during the war (37-38); and Antonia, forced by Teodora, feigns indifference toward Belisario (585-745). This, of course, is nothing new: the bibliography on role-playing in Golden Age drama is immense and, as a motif, role-playing is certainly one of the *comedia*'s defining characteristics. Fictive roles are inherently related to the notion of absence, for they serve to disguise and temporarily displace the character's "true" self for the purpose of deception.

By its very nature, role-playing exploits the difference between inner reality and outward appearance, between introspection and expression. This difference becomes explicit when Antonia, forced by Teodora to reject Belisario, complains that she is being made to express herself in a way that is directly contrary to her inner feelings: "Con el alma diré sí. / Con los labios diré no" (685-86). By virtue of their dependence upon absence, such examples of role-playing are implicitly related to the written word, itself an absential and mediated form of communication. Elias Rivers makes explicit this relation when he says that drama is a hybrid genre that is constituted by the orality of live performance as well as the written roles (*papeles*) that predetermine it (see Introduction, p. 15). It is precisely the double nature of *papeles* that makes them so potent and so dangerous.

This double nature is represented in Act II when it is decided that there will be a performance of the *Comedia de Píramo y Tisbe* at court. Much situational irony arises from this planned (metatheatrical) presentation, for there is a coincidence between the roles that the actors play in *Píramo y Tisbe* and the lives that they lead outside of it. Antonia, for example, is to play

the part of Tisbe, a role that very well reflects her real-life suf-
fering as a result of her separation from Belisario. There is a
double irony here, for this separation has been brought about
in large part by the fictional role that Teodora had forced
Antonia to play earlier: her seeming indifference to Belisario.
The coinciding of drama and life continues when Teodora
orders Filipo to play the part of Píramo (1044): out of jealousy,
the Empress has been attempting to marry Antonia off to
Filipo (497-500). Belisario, however, arrives in time to play the
role of Píramo, while Floro plays the role of his servant,
thus continuing the pattern of coinciding between fiction and
reality. Belisario realizes that playing the role of Píramo will
enable him to re-declare his love to Antonia, if nothing other
than fictively. There is great inherent irony therefore when
Belisario and Floro receive their roles (their "pieces of paper"),
according to the stage directions: "Dan un papel a cada uno"
(p. 214). Marcela's request that the women begin to rehearse
their roles is equally ironic in this context: "Ensayemos, / pues
que ya las tres sabemos / nuestros *papeles*" (1353-55). They do
indeed.

When Teodora appears, Antonia suggests that they halt their
rehearsal, for she is afraid of provoking the Empress's anger.
But Belisario craftily suggests that they merely pretend to be
rehearsing in order to express their true sentiments in a disguised manner:

> ANTONIA: Suspende un rato el ensayo
> mientras Teodora no viene,
> pues veo que conmigo tiene
> furia y violencia de un rayo.
> CAMILA: Advierte que la enojamos
> si acaso os llegase a ver.
> BELISARIO: Buen remedio: responder
> que la comedia ensayamos.
> (1372-79)

Belisario and Antonia appropriate the dramatic situation of the
Comedia de Píramo y Tisbe and exploit it as a means of secret
expression; the minute they awaken Teodora's suspicions, they
may use the excuse that they are merely reading lines from a
fictional text. The actual inscribed text of *Píramo y Tisbe* is

represented only by a few *octosílabos*, read by Floro, that do not rhyme and that are not included numerically in the verse count of Mira de Amescua's drama (between verses 1367 and 1368). Almost the entire rest of the scene is improvised by Belisario and Antonia within the general fictive situation of Píramo and Tisbe, but is expressive of their own real-life situations and feelings. This scene is similar to the final one of Act I, in which literal *papeles* (the letters read by the Emperor) also permit an oblique and secret dialogue to take place between the *privado* and Antonia.

The double nature of *papeles*—the fact that they mark the intersection between the real and the fictive—endows them with an indeterminacy that is subject to interpretation. Belisario attempts to exploit this indeterminacy in order to fool Teodora and to communicate with Antonia, but, ironically, it is Belisario himself who falls prey to it. When Antonia/Tisbe declares her love to Belisario/Píramo, the latter does not know whether her words are fiction or truth, whether it is to Tisbe or to Antonia that he is speaking:

> . . . Dí, primero,
> si es eso de tu papel,
> que ser un pecho cruel
> agora tan lisongero
> es novedad, y así infiero
> o que mi desdicha intentas
> o que a *Tisbe* representas;
> pues son tus formas ingratas,
> de Antonia cuando me matas,
> de *Tisbe* cuando me alientas.
> (1390-99; emphasis in original)

This ambivalence continues when Antonia, in her role as Tisbe, refers to a dangerous obstacle to their love:

> Píramo, en tus dulces brazos
> pudieras ver mi persona,
> si no hubiera una leona
> que nos quiere hacer pedazos;
> romper intenta los lazos
> del amor con el desdén. . . .
> (1470-75)

Tisbe referring to a "lioness" within the fictive context of the *Comedia de Píramo y Tisbe* is also Antonia referring to Teodora within a real-life one: the fictive nature of her role enables her to refer obliquely to extra-dramatic reality.

When Teodora enters and hears Belisario's accusations and Antonia's subsequent denials, Camila attempts to ease her suspicions by telling her that they are merely rehearsing their roles (1409; 1459). Teodora, however, is not so easily taken in. As in the case of the love note that she later intercepts, Teodora recognizes the hidden communication that is actually taking place. She lets this be known in no uncertain terms by making explicit the fact that she fully understands Antonia's earlier metaphorical reference to her as a "lioness":

> Basta.
> Dame ese papel, que ansí
> señal y escarmiento doy
> de que si *leona* soy
> habéis de temblar de mí.
> (1489-93; emphasis in original)

Teodora grabs the written text of the *Comedia de Píramo y Tisbe* and rips it up in an act that parallels Justinian's when, near the beginning of the drama, he rips up the blank sheet that Fabricio had unknowingly handed him as a testimony to his valor at war (447). However, whereas the Emperor was deceived by appearances that were backed up by proof that is inscribed on *papel*, Teodora is much less trusting: she is not taken in by *papeles* of any kind. Her act of ripping up the *comedia*—like that evoked by Antonia of the lioness who wants to make *pedazos* of Píramo and Tisbe and "break the ties of their love" (see above)—is a powerfully violent image for the disjunction of the fictive context that has helped to establish a secret communicative contact between the two lovers. It is also a self-referential gesture on the part of the drama itself: not only does Teodora disrupt and literally fragment the *Comedia de Píramo y Tisbe*, she has precisely the same violently disruptive function throughout Mira de Amescua's drama.

The farce is over, as Floro acknowledges in words that reinforce the coincidence of fictive drama and life: "La comedia se acabó. / Perdón, ilustre senado" (1498-99). Although these verses are from the *Comedia de Píramo y Tisbe*, they are equally applicable to the extra-dramatic reality, that is, the represented world of Mira de Amescua's *El ejemplo mayor de la desdicha*. One proof of this is that these lines, unlike the others that had been read aloud earlier, *are* included in the verse-count of Mira's drama: that is, they mark the intersection between the fictive and the real. These closing words of *Píramo and Tisbe* (and, significantly, of this scene) exemplify the ambivalent reality that is implied by the word *papel*. Act II of *El ejemplo* is dominated by this "play within the play" that, by virtue of its inherent ambivalence (reality or role?), allows oblique and figurative reference.

Aside from the numerous appearances of actual written texts, there are in *El ejemplo* several figurative references to textuality. Belisario, for example, meditates upon his own rise and fall in terms that recapitulate both the "textual" and the "visual" motifs:

> *Lee* en mis ojos los sucesos
> de los mortales, y *mira*
> las vueltas de la fortuna
> en mis calientes cenizas.
>
> (2680-83)

He later refers to himself as "fábula y risa / de la fortuna" (2719-20). *Autoridades*'s fifth definition of the term *fábula* is the most obviously applicable here: "Metaphoricamente se toma por irrisión, quando se dice que uno está hecho fábula de todos, esto es objeto de la irrisión de todos." But the second definition is of equal interest, for it has a specifically textual dimension: "Se toma tambien por ficcion artificiosa, con que se procura encubrir u disimular alguna verdad philosophica o moral." This definition implies a blending of fiction and truth that is implicitly reinforced by the duality of Belisario's status. Both his "fictive" rise to power and his "real" fall from it are subsumed by the text of his life, a *fábula* that is itself an extended metaphor for a deeper truth, namely, the inconstancy of Fate.

Fate's mutability is, of course, one of the defining motifs of the *tragedias de privanza*, and it is certainly central to this drama. In his earlier-mentioned study of the *tragedias de privanza*, Raymond MacCurdy makes the case that although *El ejemplo* has a great deal of tragic pathos, it is by no means a great, or even a good, tragedy:

> Unmerited punishment is, of course, a major source of tragic pathos. But a "good" moral and "good" pathos do not necessarily make a good tragedy. Even though Mira de Amescua's play avoids the easy moral of poetic justice, it is hard to forget that the hero's catastrophe and the lesson to be learned from it were produced by the scheming—during three acts—of a spiteful woman. (166)

Although I concede that *El ejemplo* does not represent the greatest tragedy that the Golden Age has to offer, it *does* have many fine moments of pathos and poetry. I do not believe that its tragic dimensions can be written off simply because they ". . . were produced by the scheming . . . of a spiteful woman." There is much in the drama to suggest that Teodora should not be read in so limited a fashion. The true source of "tragic pathos" in Mira de Amescua's play—as in all *dramas de privanza*—is the mutability of Fortune. It is precisely in regard to such mutability that Teodora takes on real importance because she is the principal human medium through which Fortune manifests itself, particularly in her relation to Belisario. In fact, the drama implicitly makes her into something of the embodiment of Fortune by emphasizing the fact that mutability is her defining characteristic.

Early in Act I, for example, when Belisario learns from Leoncio that a woman had ordered his assassination, he makes an observation that is a misogynistic commonplace of Golden Age literature and that has a very long tradition, namely, that the essence of woman is her mutability:

> En todo tiene mudanza
> su fácil naturaleza,
> y sólo *tiene* firmeza
> en el odio y la venganza.
> (169-72; emphasis in original)

Belisario immediately goes on to identify this inconstancy with Fate itself:

> ¡Ay miserable pensión
> de la vida! ¡Ay hado fiero!

> El triunfo y pompa que espero
> es la rueda del pavón.
>
> (173-76)

As soon as Teodora makes her first appearance, she refers to the mutability of her feelings about Belisario: "Bien le quise y mal le quiero" (488). When Belisario returns from war, near the beginning of Act II, Teodora's attitude has once again changed:

> ¡Ayer tanto aborrecer
> y hoy amor tan singular!
> Bien dicen que es como el mar
> el alma de una mujer.
>
> (1998-2001)

Belisario is therefore incredulous when Teodora begins to flirt with him by dropping a ribbon:

> ¿Con qué intención
> la banda dejó caer?
> ¡que pas[e] así una mujer
> del rigor a la afición,
> tal fácilmente!
>
> (2078-82)

But her love turns to hatred when she perceives that Belisario has once again rejected her advances:

> Amor, no fuistes amor.
> Sin duda fuistes deseo,
> pues que ansí trocado os veo
> segunda vez en rigor.
> Declaré mi voluntad.
> Despreció me; es mi enemigo.
>
> (2142-47)

With regard to Belisario, Teodora clearly represents a volatile flux from one emotional extreme to the other.

She is also implicitly identified at various points with Fortune or Fate. During the *Comedia de Píramo y Tisbe*, when Belisario, in his role as Píramo, speaks of "envious Fortune" (1462), we know that he is referring obliquely to Teodora. Antonia in her role as Tisbe likewise complains that *el hado* divides the two lovers (1488). We may see now, in retrospect, that Teodora embodies arbitrary Fortune, which manifests itself in *El ejemplo* primarily by way of violent disjunction on various levels. She effects a communicative disjunction between certain characters, such as Belisario and Antonia and, later, between Belisario and Justinian. Her personal attempt against Belisario's life causes Justinian to protect him by literally dividing the institutional symbols of the Empire, thus creating a disjunction on the symbolic level of civil order. On the level of language, Teodora embodies a radical disjunction between signifiers and their conventionally related signifieds that results in the protagonist's symbolic blindness. This pattern of disjunction reaches its appropriate culmination with the literal and violent separation of Belisario's eyes from his head.

Teodora's relation to Fortune is obviously important to the whole question of communicative subversion and, of course, writing. This is demonstrated in each of the three acts. In Act I, she inverts and disrupts the conventional sign system by making indifference the only way that Antonia can express her love to Belisario. In Act II, she literally rips up the communicative context that allows the expression of secret and figurative meanings: the *Comedia de Píramo y Tisbe*. In Act III, she intercepts Belisario's note to Antonia, thus rupturing the (written) communicative context. This final subversion is, of course, the most devastating, for Teodora retains its traces—the note itself—only to recontextualize them in order to fool Justinian and effect her vengeance.

There is a logical progression in these three different communicative contexts that are, in turn, subverted by Teodora: *oral; oral+written; written*. The first context, in which Antonia is forced to reject Belisario, is essentially oral. It depends upon presence: spoken words, physical gestures, facial movements. The second is the *Comedia de Píramo y Tisbe*, a context that, like all dramatic art, is a hybrid of the oral and the written. The third communicative context, the note sent by Belisario to Antonia, is (obviously) written. She uses this final disruption to bring about the hero's downfall. In *El ejemplo mayor de la desdicha*, it is precisely written texts—their closed and secret quality, their essential *drift*, their theoretically infinite potential for recontextualization and reinterpretation—that best manifest the arbitrariness and mutability of Fate itself.

Chapter Four

Dangerous Scripts in Tirso's
Cautela contra cautela

A motif common to *La estrella de Sevilla* and to Mira de
Amescua's *El ejemplo mayor de la desdicha*, as well as to much
Spanish literature of the seventeenth century, is the contrast
between appearances and reality, between signs and the meanings that they traditionally denote. In the language of structuralist linguistics, such an opposition constitutes a disjunction
between a signifier and signified that under normal circumstances are bound together by convention. This undercutting of
linguistic and other sign systems is often exploited in the
comedia for the purposes of deception and transgression. As
Catherine Larson correctly notes in her recent study: "the
comedia depends upon willed ambiguity and linguistic misfir-
ing to create conflict . . . . many of its characters 'read' incorrectly;
their false assumptions, misinterpretations, and unproven alle-
gations fuel the fires of the dramatic conflict" (138).

In *La estrella de Sevilla*, for example, it is precisely under
the pretext of *honoring* the citizens of Seville that King Sancho
effectively *dishonors* them; in *El ejemplo mayor de la desdicha*,
Teodora falsely accuses Belisario of crimes that she herself has
committed and thereby effects his downfall and death. Like *El
ejemplo*, Tirso de Molina's *Cautela contra cautela* (1621) concerns itself with the courtly intrigue implied by *privanza* and
similarly dramatizes a disjunction between signifiers and their
conventionally related signifieds. But whereas the discrepancy
between appearances and reality is only one of several essential motifs in both Mira de Amescua's play and *La estrella de
Sevilla*, it generates nearly all of the action in Tirso's. Like Mira
de Amescua's *El ejemplo*, this drama has received scant critical attention.[1]

Cautela has two lines of action. The primary (political)

intrigue begins when King Alfonso of Naples receives an anonymous written warning about a conspiracy against his reign. He concocts a plan by which the warning may be verified: he and his closest advisor, Enrique de Avalos, publicly pretend that the latter has fallen from the King's graces, in the hope that any possible conspirators will attempt to persuade him to join their cause. The ruse is successful, for the conspirators—the Prince of Taranto, the Prince of Salerno, and Ludovico (one of Enrique's closest friends)—do just that. When the conspirators accidentally discover that Enrique's apparent fall was nothing but a ruse, they attempt to convince the King that *their* conspiracy was also a ruse designed to entrap Enrique, whom they accuse of treason. Through a series of misleading appearances, King Alfonso comes to believe their false accusation, but tragedy is narrowly averted when Enrique manages to prove his innocence and the conspirators are brought to justice.

The secondary (love) intrigue is, as usual, far simpler: Enrique is initially attracted to two countesses, one wealthy—Elena—and the other poor—Porcia. Through a series of misleading circumstances, he becomes convinced that Elena loves him sincerely and that Porcia's love is strictly mercenary. Ironically, Enrique has reversed the reality of the situation, for it is Porcia's love and not Elena's which is sincere. It is only in the drama's final scene that the truth is revealed and he is betrothed to Porcia.

Cautela's action faithfully adheres to Alexander Parker's classic formulation of a structure that is characteristic of many *comedias*:

> The normal criterion of unity of action must be replaced by that of unity of theme, and it is in this way that the apparent duality of many Spanish plays is resolved. In those that have two plots, a main plot and a subplot with different actions or with a different dramatic tone, the relation of the one plot to the other must be looked for in the relation of each to the theme. ("Spanish" 685)

In the case of *Cautela contra cautela*, what unifies the two plots is the fact that both deal in different ways with the nature and limits of perception: the fact that reality is often hidden by deceptive appearances.

This idea makes itself felt in the drama's opening scene when Enrique points out the contrast between his official, public function as *marqués* (and court favorite) and the amorous activities in which he secretly indulges as a private citizen:

> Don Alfonso de Aragón,
> Rey de Nápoles, confía
> de la diligencia mía,
> con una inmensa afición,
> este reino: gran privado,
> Ministro, por tales modos
> he de dar ejemplo a todos.
> ¿Qué mucho que recatado
> salga yo por la ciudad
> de noche a barrios señores,
> si aunque son todos amores,
> mostrarlos es liviandad?
>
> (917a-b)[2]

Enrique's words also emphasize the contrast between day and night: in order to maintain the secrecy of certain acts, they should be performed under the covering obscurity of night. This notion is prevalent throughout. When King Alfonso first suggests his strategy for discovering the conspirators' identities, for example, he contrasts the secret realities of night with the apparent realities of daytime by declaring that although he and Enrique will maintain their friendship, from that point on, they will see one another only by night:

> Vendrásme de noche a ver:
> seré tu amigo de noche;
> y aunque siempre lo seré,
> engañaremos de día
> el humano parecer.
>
> (926a)

Likewise, when the conspirators visit Enrique in his home, they do so at night in order to avoid notice. Once they have concluded their business, the Prince of Taranto cautions against their staying too long, for fear that the light of day will reveal their plans:

> Quédese para otro día
> la sesión en este estado;

que pienso que ya ha llorado
sus perlas el alba fría,
y importa que no nos vean
para que no se publique.

(943b)

The opposition of day and night is, of course, related to that of light and darkness. When Alfonso first begins to suspect Enrique of disloyalty, he expresses his doubts in the following way: "¿Qué sombras / son éstas, que a la amistad / turban la luz generosa?" (952a-b). Shadows and darkness have much the same function in *Cautela* as in *El ejemplo mayor de la desdicha*: they represent the limits of human perception, the inability to see hidden realities. Enrique's servant Chirimía refers to this human fallibility in the drama's opening scene when he questions the relation that Enrique has with his two closest friends, Ludovico and César: ". . . no sabe el poderoso / cuál es su amigo de veras; / qué amistad hay verdadera" (918a). Not even the most powerful of men, the servant claims, should assume that appearances are faithful indicators of the reality of a given situation.

The ambivalence of appearances in *Cautela* inspires the need to verify or test them. Enrique wishes, for example, to test the two women to whom he is attracted. He therefore asks his two closest friends, Ludovico and César, to accompany him in order that they might listen to and pass judgment on the women's responses as he addresses them separately. By registering the women's reactions and by listening to his friends' opinions, Enrique hopes to learn which woman loves him more sincerely. While speaking to Elena, however, he accidentally calls her "Porcia"; she immediately dismisses him and indignantly retires, despite his protestations (921a). Enrique then decides to test Porcia by calling *her* by a name other than her own; that is, he will do intentionally with her what was accidental in the case of Elena (921b). But Porcia's love is unconditional: so sincere that she feels no need to verify *his* feelings for her. Her words thereby constitute an implicit chastising of Enrique's own need to verify: "Amaros me toca a mí; / no me toca averiguar / si soy amada de vos" (923a).

The contrast between appearance and reality is also central to the disagreement between Enrique's two servants, Julio and Chirimía, in the drama's opening scene. When Chirimía asks

Enrique whether Ludovico or César is more loyal to him, Julio defends Ludovico:

> Certifico
> que pienso que Ludovico
> ha hecho demostración
> de amigo más verdadero:
> lenguas se hace en alabarte.
>
> (918a)

The utter indirectness of Julio's statement renders it somewhat dubious, for, rather than stating simply and directly that Ludovico is the truer friend, he *certifies* that he *thinks* that Ludovico has made a *demonstration* of being the truer friend. This obliqueness implicitly undercuts his apparent intention of convincing Enrique of Ludovico's loyalty. It is clear that Tirso is here sacrificing verisimilitude of characterization in the name of a thematics that is more central to the drama as a whole, namely, the opposition between words and deeds as well as that between appearances and reality.

Julio defends Ludovico by saying that the latter has verbally praised Enrique at every opportunity. But it is on precisely the same grounds that Chirimía attacks Ludovico, that is, by claiming that his words are nothing more than an outward show:

> ¡Qué poco sabes del arte
> de un amigo lisonjero!
> Si deso te satisfaces,
> en él la amistad se acaba:
> siempre Ludovico alaba
> lo que dices, lo que haces,
> lo que comes, lo que bebes,
> lo que calzas, lo que vistes,
> lo que ríes; y son chistes,
> motes y sentencias breves
> cuanto arrojas por los labios,
> aunque necedades sean.
> *Y amigos que lisonjean,*
> *ni son amigos, ni sabios.*
>
> (918a)

Chirimía disparages the kind of friendship that consists in mere words of praise, prior to defending César as the more loyal of the two:

> Mira, y con ojos serenos
> a César siempre verás:
> *sin duda te quiere más,*
> *pues es quien te alaba menos.*
>
> (918a)

Chirimía is, in short, something of a cynic when it comes to language, for he argues that César praises Enrique less and therefore must love him more. His implied argument is very simple: as ostensible signs, words prove nothing in and of themselves and, depending upon the context, may actually denote the opposite of that which they appear to mean.

The contrast between sign and meaning, as well as that between style and substance, continues in the following scene when Enrique describes the paradox of loving two women at the same time. Ludovico does not express any opinion about *what* Enrique has said; instead, he praises Enrique's elegantly poetic mode of expression: "¡Divinamente ha pintado / sus efectos Vuexcelencia! / ¡Qué discreción! ¡Qué elocuencia!" (919a). In contrast to Ludovico, César ignores Enrique's style of expression and comments instead on its substance. Like Chirimía, César is more interested in reality than in appearance, in substantive meaning as opposed to its mode of expression. He therefore contradicts Enrique by telling him that his feelings constitute a mere inclination, not true love (919a-b).

When Enrique and his two friends arrive at Elena's house and hear her speak, Ludovico immediately praises her eloquent manner of expression: "Divinamente arguyó" (920a). These words echo his earlier praise of Enrique's eloquence, and his second use of the term *divinamente* to characterize Elena's rhetoric serves to underline this parallel. He claims that Elena sincerely loves Enrique (920b); but when Enrique asks César's opinion, the latter once again disagrees with Ludovico. As in the case of Enrique's *inclinación*, César remains unconvinced that Elena's love is real. When Enrique asks him to justify his opinion, César responds by attacking precisely what Ludovico had praised, namely, Elena's smoothly rhetorical manner of speaking: "En que lo dice muy bien. / Más tiene de vizcaíno / el amor que de elocuente" (920b). True love, César argues, does not express itself well.

When Enrique mistakenly calls Elena "Porcia," it is an

explicit example of the disjunction between sign and referent, the lack of "fit" between words and the world. When Elena angrily dismisses him as a result of this error, César further denies the sincerity of her feelings by claiming that true love does not know how to complain. He emphasizes the hollow nature of Elena's sentiments by noting that such shows of jealousy are merely the appearance, the outer signs, of love and not its reality:

> Celos te quiso *ostentar*
> porque *muestras* de amor son,
> y a tan ligera ocasión
> cogió el copete.
>
> (921b)

César's concept of love is as an ideal and transcendent constant that is indifferent to eloquent modes of expression.

This rather metaphysical concept of love reappears when Enrique goes to visit Porcia. He addresses her and hyperbolically praises her beauty with a series of poetic conceits that are typical of the courtly love tradition, but Porcia claims to be insulted rather than complimented by such rhetoric, and proceeds to chastise him:

> No me hagáis tales agravios:
> *en palabras más sencillas*
> *se explica amor verdadero*;
> bien mi desengaño alcanza
> que no tengo otra alabanza,
> sino que por veros muero.
> Alabadme de constante,
> y *no me alabéis de hermosa*,
> *que es lisonja sospechosa*.
>
> (922a)

She clearly echoes César's sentiments in this opinion and, like him, explicitly valorizes interior transcendent reality over exterior appearance when she asks to be praised for the constancy of her love rather than for her physical beauty.

When César claims that Porcia's love is sincere, Ludovico disagrees—as might be expected—on the basis of her lack of eloquence: "habla muy caseramente. / Pienso que es tibio su amor" (922b). In his argument against Porcia's sincerity, Ludovico values style and appears to assume a motivated relation between the richness of the signifier and the signified it denotes. Porcia, he argues, expresses her love commonly, and her love therefore must likewise be "lukewarm." Ludovico had already expressed misgivings about Porcia at the beginning of the scene: because she is poor, he feels that her only motivation is economic and claims that what she really wants from Enrique is a jewel: "Más quisiera alguna joya" (922b). This is an ironic anticipation of the jewel that Porcia does in fact receive from Elena after requesting money from her, in Act II (935-36). The irony consists in the fact that this jewel will serve to confirm that Porcia's love of Enrique is unconditional and altruistic, rather than selfish, as Ludovico claims, for the minute she receives it from Elena, she sends it to Enrique so as to help him in what she believes is his hour of need.

When Enrique proceeds deliberately to call Porcia by a name other than her own, she—in clear contrast to Elena—does not complain. Ludovico interprets this as a sign that she does not truly love: "No se quejó; no es amante" (923b). In this way, he manages to convince Enrique that Elena loves him more sincerely. The name that Enrique chooses to call Porcia "mistakenly"—Casandra—signals the pattern of her inability to communicate her love to Enrique: similar to the case of Aeschylus's Cassandra (who was destined to speak the truth and yet never be believed), Porcia's various expressions of love go unbelieved by Enrique in this scene, as will similar protestations, until the drama's final scene.

Enrique's incorrect conclusion that Elena loves him more sincerely than Porcia leads him to other, equally incorrect conclusions. Soon after he begins pretending to have fallen from Alfonso's graces, as per the King's orders, a messenger comes to inform him that a certain countess wishes to see him, but the messenger leaves before he may be asked her identity. Enrique erroneously concludes that the unnamed countess must be Elena:

> De Elena debe de ser,
> que el enojo de los celos
> serenó con mis desdichas.

> Porcia, como pobre, entiendo
> que mi estado pretendía,
> y ya habrá dado a los vientos
> su esperanza y su cuidado.

> (934a)

Enrique unknowingly and ironically reverses the truth of the matter by ascribing selfishly material motivations to Porcia and altruistic ones to Elena. The irony of Enrique's mistaken sense of reality becomes explicit in the next scene when Elena reveals privately to her servant that her "love" for the *privado* was in fact motivated by nothing other than personal ambition:

> Nunca supe qué es amor:
> y *aquel fingido cuidado*
> *era una razón de estado*
> *y desinio superior.*
> *Hablando afecto, no amaba*;
> mi aumento así pretendía,
> porque ser mujer quería
> del que este reino mandaba.
> Cayó, y así te prometo
> que mi intención hizo pausa,
> porque cesando la causa,
> ha de cesar el efecto.

> (934b)

Elena's "hablando afecto, no amaba" perfectly exemplifies the "emptying out" of language, the dangerous discrepancy between material signifiers (words) and the conceptual signifieds (meanings) to which they are conventionally assigned.[3]

Enrique's mistaken judgment that the unnamed countess who wishes to see him is Elena is reinforced by yet another misapprehension, when a messenger arrives bearing a note and a package from an unnamed countess, but again leaves before he may be asked the name of the sender (939a). By analogy with the case of the other note, Enrique again concludes that Elena has sent this one. He mistakenly ascribes the sender's anonymity to Elena's sense of discretion:

> Finezas serán de Elena,
> que hoy con discreto cuidado,

en su amor disimulado
embozó también la pena.

(939a-b)

In this case, however, Enrique is not totally to blame, for the package's contents and accompanying letter constitute visible objective signs that powerfully reinforce his mistaken assumption. The letter contains an explicit declaration of constant love and describes the nature of the contents of the package, but is unsigned. As in the case of Belisario's unsigned note to Antonia in *El ejemplo mayor de la desdicha*, the author is identified by way of handwriting. When Enrique reads it, he immediately recognizes the handwriting as Elena's, and when Chirimía asks whether the author has signed it, he confidently replies that a signature is unnecessary:

Cuando viene a ser
de una persona querida
la letra tan parecida
la firma no es necesaria.

(939b)

Unbeknownst to him, Porcia had accidentally injured her hand upon hearing the shocking news of Enrique's ostensible fall from power. When she requested money from Elena to send to Enrique, and Elena responded by giving her the jewel, Porcia wished to send an explanatory note along with it. Physically unable to write, Porcia then requested that Elena write out the words that she (Porcia) would dictate. Likewise, when Enrique opens the package and sees several jewels, he recognizes one of them as belonging to Elena: "Yo vi / en su pecho aquesta joya" (940a). The letter and the jewels together constitute the most explicit example in *Cautela* of the discrepancy between appearances and reality, for they appear to point to Elena but are in fact expressions of Porcia's love.

Implicit in this discrepancy is the contrast between strictly material signifiers, consistently associated with Elena, and their more transcendent signifieds, consistently associated with Porcia. This pattern first manifests itself by way of the two women's relative economic ("material") status: Elena's wealth and Porcia's poverty. The graphic marks that Elena has put on the page in performing the physical act of inscription stand in contrast to the spoken *razones* dictated to her by Porcia, whose thoughts and feelings they represent. Enrique himself declares that the jewels' true value lies not in their material worth, but rather in ". . . la fineza / de la mujer que las da" (940a). He praises the constancy of true love while deprecating its merely material manifestations, but ironically ascribes that constancy to Elena, the woman for whom personal and material gain are the only motivations.

Elena redirects her attention to Ludovico once she hears the news of Enrique's fall from power. Enrique, however, remains deceived by appearances until near the very end of the drama, when King Alfonso reveals to him Elena's desire to marry the newly advanced Ludovico (959a). At this point, Enrique indignantly confronts Elena by asking about the jewel and the letter:

> ENRIQUE: ¿Este papel no es de Elena?
> ELENA: La *letra* sí, las *razones*
> de Porcia son.
> ENRIQUE: ¿Pues no era
> esta joya tuya?
> ELENA: Sí,
> mas dísela a Porcia.
>
> (959a-b)

Once the truth of the matter is revealed, Chirimía advises Enrique to marry Porcia (959b).

To summarize: the secondary love intrigue is wholly generated by a contrast between appearance and reality, a disjunction between material signifiers and their signifieds. Enrique is confronted by a series of signs that are essentially misleading, for they represent a state of affairs that is directly opposed to the reality of the situation, that is, *parecer* is radically opposed to *ser*.[4] The opposition between Elena and Porcia in their relation to Enrique is paralleled by that of two other contrasting pairs of characters who are also intimately involved with the protagonist, his servants (Julio and Chirimía), and his friends (Ludovico and César). These character oppositions manifest themselves in much the same terms: material versus transcendent value, ornate versus plain speaking, selfishness versus altruism, exteriority versus interiority, form versus content, signifier versus signified. By exhibiting the deceptive and arbitrary relation of physical signs to the reality that they ostensibly represent, the secondary plot constitutes a consistent metaphysical valorization of the signified and an equivalent devaluation of the signifier.

This metaphysics is explicit in the verses quoted above that reveal to Enrique that the written *letra* (an exterior, explicitly physical sign) is Elena's, but that the spoken *razones* (the interior constancy of true love) are Porcia's. This valorization is typified by the opposition between oral and written communication. As the signifier of a signified that is itself a signifier (the spoken word), writing appears to be doubly removed from the reality that it ostensibly represents. The potentially distorting aspect of the written supplement is fully exhibited by the misleading letter that Enrique receives, a letter that absolutely belies the *logos* (Porcia's oral discourse) that is its source.

The discrepancy between sign and conventional meaning generates, as we have seen, much of the action of *Cautela*'s secondary plot. In the primary (political) plot, this same discrepancy is manifested specifically in terms of writing in both literal and figurative senses. In *El ejemplo mayor de la desdicha*, we remember, Teodora causes and utilizes disjunction in various communicative contexts throughout. In the last of these contexts, she exploits the drift of the written word—its explicit lack of a determined and particular communicative context—by recontextualizing a note written by Belisario. In *Cautela contra cautela*, the note that Enrique receives is a clear example of the *drift* that is inherent in all written texts, for it is not merely ambivalent in regard to the context of its production, it is downright misleading. *Cautela*'s primary plot revolves around the motif of inscription, which has much the same potential *drift* that we have seen in other dramas examined thus far.

The first example of written texts appears in Act I, when two *pretendientes* appear at the palace in order to present petitions to King Alfonso (924b). The link between royalty and inscription that we have seen in other dramas is thereby immediately established. Alfonso immediately begins to carry out official business by having his *privado* read aloud to him the documents on his desk (925a). One of the papers that Enrique reads aloud is the anonymous warning about the conspiracy:

"Señor,
otro aviso te dio ayer
el que este escribe a tu Alteza.
Mira, Alfonso Aragonés,
que se conjuran, y tratan
de quitarte el reino, tres
Príncipes vasallos tuyos:
y el que escribe este papel
no osa declararte más."

(925a)

This unsigned warning is as important to *Cautela*'s primary plot
as is Juan Labrador's inscribed epitaph in *El villano en su
rincón* and King Sancho's written guarantee of freedom to the
slave girl in *La estrella de Sevilla*: the act of reading instigates
all of the action that follows.

Alfonso reveals to Enrique that he has already received several similar warnings but always doubted their veracity because
he cannot believe that anyone would conspire against (what he
considers) a just reign and because of the absence and anonymity of their author. The author's absence is all the more
evident on a purely linguistic level, for he stylistically absents
himself from the text of his letter by referring to himself in the
third person rather than in the first person, identifying himself only as "he who has written this paper." We have already
seen the potential dangers of anonymous notes in the secondary intrigue.

Enrique defends the possibility that there is truth to the warnings, for any number of individuals might oppose Alfonso's
reign on the basis that he is not native to Naples, a point
explicitly emphasized by the fact that the note is addressed to
"Alfonso Aragonés." Enrique adds that the warnings should not
be doubted merely because of their author's anonymity, which
might theoretically be justified by his need to protect himself
or to conform to a situation that is implicitly contradictory:

Si el nombre no declaró
quien te avisa, puede ser
que no se atreva, o que sea
de los conjurados él,
por amistad o violencia;
y así para no romper
la ley de su juramento

> ni ser un vasallo infiel,
> desta manera te avisa.
>
> (925b)

By implying a variety of possible interpretations, the note suggests the potential reversibility of appearances that is evident throughout the secondary line of action. According to Enrique, inscription is the means whereby the author of these warnings may hypothetically be both a loyal vassal *and* true to his oath of conspiracy.

Alfonso therefore suggests his strategy of acting out the fiction that Enrique has fallen from grace. We have already seen a similarly explicit example of fictional playacting in *El ejemplo mayor de la desdicha*: the presentation of the *Comedia de Píramo y Tisbe*. Unlike Mira de Amescua's play, which utilizes the explicitly fictional play within the play to reinforce the drama's principal action, *Cautela contra cautela* utilizes such metatheater in a far more important way, for King Alfonso's *cautela* and the fiction that it inspires Ludovico and the conspirators to utilize in reaction actually constitute the essential action, as announced by the drama's title.[5]

As Elias Rivers's article on Calderón reminds us, all such examples of theatricality are intimately connected with inscription: the written *papeles* that underlie the oral *roles* that actors represent (see Introduction, p. 15). At the beginning of *Cautela*, King Alfonso receives an anonymous *papel* warning him of a possible threat to his reign. His actions are directed at verifying or disproving it. In order to accomplish this he himself becomes a "writer" or "playwright" who creates roles (*papeles*) for himself and Enrique. Alfonso's "script" duplicates the essential action of every *drama de privanza* of seventeenth-century Spain, that is, a minister's or favorite's fall from the graces of his king. But because this fall is artificially created by one of the drama's characters, because it is a self-consciously fictional part of the "true" action of *Cautela*, it is rendered ironic by the drama as a whole. For this reason, Tirso's *Cautela contra cautela* constitutes a unique entity in Golden Age drama. It is not a *drama de privanza* (like *El ejemplo*), but a *metadrama de privanza*. It is an examination, not only of the psychology and status of the institution of *privanza*, but also, self-referentially, of the theatrical (and implicitly metatheatrical) mode by which this institution finds expression throughout seventeenth-century Spain.

Another important function of *Cautela*'s metatheater is to reiterate the motif that is so prevalent in the drama's secondary plot: the contrast between appearances and reality, between ostensible signifiers and their conventional signifieds. King Alfonso attempts to exploit Enrique's apparent fall in order to fool others and to test their loyalty. He expresses his motives for such a test in a way that explicitly echoes Chirimía's earlier words about knowing who one's friends and enemies are and that recapitulates Enrique's own motives for testing the love of Elena and Porcia:

> Una cautela pensé
> con que tú puedas sabello.
> Yo me acuerdo que una vez
> me dijiste que felice
> solo ha de llamarse aquel
> que supiere cuatro cosas:
> qué amigo le quiere bien,
> qué dama le corresponde,
> qué criado le es fiel,
> qué enemigo le persigue.
>
> (926a)

The *cautela* will test the loyalty of the people surrounding both Alfonso and Enrique, for, just as Enrique will be in a position to learn who is unfaithful to Alfonso, so will Alfonso be in a position to see who is unfaithful to Enrique.

Papel appears again soon after Enrique's ostensible fall when Ludovico delivers a note to him from Alfonso. Enrique recognizes the royal seal and places the letter on his head in a gesture of respect (931b).[6] Once he has read the letter, Enrique writes out a response and hands it to Ludovico with the following words: "Pídeme el Rey dos *papeles*, / y así donde están le aviso" (932a). With these words, Enrique claims to be telling Alfonso (in the very letter he hands to Ludovico) the whereabouts of two *papeles*. In fact, the two *papeles* to which he refers are the letter itself and the *papel* (role) of fallen favorite that he is currently acting out at Alfonso's behest. Enrique makes explicit the duplicity of the term *papel* and thereby self-reflexively exemplifies its potential ambivalence.

Enrique more radically exploits linguistic ambivalence when the princes ask him to join in their conspiracy to hand Naples over to King Carlos VIII of France. When Enrique had received word that two princes would soon come to visit him (930b), he immediately informed Alfonso, who has secretly hidden himself in the *privado*'s home. The entire scene is therefore contextualized by Alfonso's secret presence. Enrique's spoken oath, ostensibly directed at the absent French King Carlos, has different meanings for his present audience (the conspirators) and his "absent" and hidden one (King Alfonso):

> Famoso Rey, en quien puedo
> decir que oyéndome estás,
> pues con una firma das
> mercedes, honor y miedo:
> mi Rey eres, y protesto
> que, aunque aventure mi honor
> y me tengan por traidor,
> te obedezco y sirvo en esto.
> Oyeme, Rey liberal,
> si aquí alcanza tu poder:
> yo te prometo de ser
> eternamente leal.
> Este cargo que he aceptado,
> en servicio tuyo fue,
> porque a mi lealtad y fe
> ningún vasallo ha igualado.
> Recibe, Rey, mi deseo,
> pues puedo decir que aquí
> estás, y me escuchas.
>
> (943a)

For the hidden Alfonso, it is the faithful *privado* who utters this oath; for the conspirators, it is the vengeful *caído*. Enrique adroitly utilizes language that allows the two contradictory levels of fiction and reality to subsist and intermix, much as we saw in certain verses from the *Comedia de Píramo y Tisbe*, the drama within the drama of Mira de Amescua's *El ejemplo* (see above, pp. 83-87).

When Enrique addresses an unnamed king with the modality of presence inherent in oral communication ("oyéndome estás . . . Oyeme, Rey liberal, . . . puedo decir que aquí / estás, y me escuchas"), the conspirators assume that he is invoking the French monarch Carlos VIII and making him present in a purely figurative sense. But his words are also more literally addressed to another king who is present despite his apparent absence. The ambivalence of Enrique's words allows him to play his assigned role as *caído* (and now traitor), yet still remain loyal to his king. In this respect, we now see that his earlier speculation about the author of the anonymous warnings to King Alfonso ("para no romper / la ley de su juramento / ni ser un vasallo infiel, / desta manera te avisa" [925b]) was an anticipation of his own rather paradoxical position at this juncture. Both he and the anonymous author utilize ambivalent *papeles* (in different senses) to aid King Alfonso.

Enrique again exploits purposefully ambivalent language when he swears secrecy to the conspirators:

> juro, y digo que este intento
> de mi boca no sabrán,
> *sino solo los que están*
> *oyendo mi juramento.*
> Juro por Dios trino y uno
> so pena de que esta espada
> en mi sangre esté manchada,
> de no tratar con ninguno,
> *fuera de aquellos que estamos*
> *presentes*, nuestra intención
> y aquesta conjuración.
>
> (943a-b)

King Alfonso is, in fact, listening and present. This ambivalence results in a great sense of irony for the audience, who, along with Enrique and Alfonso, can thoroughly enjoy the exclusion of the conspirators from the hidden sense of the *privado*'s words.[7]

Linguistic ambivalence again appears near the beginning of Act III when the King addresses Ludovico and the two princes. Like Enrique before him, Alfonso uses language that implies a meaning that is obviously apparent to himself and to the audience, but not to the conspirators. The princes invoke all they have done on the King's behalf:

> TARANTO: Es que ve tu Majestad
> mis acciones.
> REY: Sí las veo.

107

```
SALERNO:   Y es que mi amor ha sabido
           tu Majestad.
REY:                 Sí lo sé.
TARANTO:   Nadie nos iguala en fe
           ni amor.
REY:                 Ansí lo he entendido.
                                    (946b)
```

Alfonso's responses are highly ironic in that they potentially
signify the opposite of that which they appear to signify. The
same may be said of his exchange with Ludovico just after this
one, in which both speakers engage in a duplicity that is made
explicit by the King's aside:

```
LUDOVICO:   Lo que los tres deseamos
            te suceda.
REY: (Aparte.)          No permita
            mi fortuna tal suceso.
      (Alto.)   Y vosotros, antes deso,
            tengáis lo que os solicita
            mi cuidado.
                                    (947a)
```

Given what Alfonso has learned through his *cautela* and given
Ludovico's intentions, the actual (as opposed to the expressed)
desires of both parties are obvious to the audience.[8]

The potential dangers of such role-playing, we remember,
are exemplified in *El ejemplo mayor de la desdicha*, when
Belisario suggests to Antonia that they use the ambivalence of
their roles in the rehearsal of the *Comedia de Píramo y Tisbe*
to communicate secretly with one another. In attempting to
deceive the jealous Teodora, however, Belisario is himself
deceived: when he addresses Antonia in his role as Píramo,
he does not know whether it is Antonia or Tisbe who is
responding.

Likewise, in *Cautela*, Enrique is deceived when he enters the
King's chamber and Alfonso speaks angrily to him. The *privado* is unaware of Ludovico's presence behind a curtain,
where Alfonso had sent him to read royal business aloud to him
and where he intently observes their every move. Alfonso is
playing his role as wrathful king speaking to an unfaithful
caído, but Enrique is unaware of Ludovico's hidden presence
and consequently believes that the monarch's anger is real:

"Nadie nos ve: ¡estando a solas, / me trata el Rey desta suerte!"
(948a). When Alfonso realizes that Enrique is taking him
seriously, he dismisses Ludovico and reminds his *privado* of
the roles they must play:

> Siempre que muestre contigo
> tal enojo, considera
> que *soy tu Rey por defuera,*
> y que *dentro soy tu amigo.*
> Si dentro en mi pecho estás,
> llave es mi amor con que abras:
> *no mires, no, mis palabras;*
> *el alma has de ver no más.*
>
> (949a-b)

Alfonso evokes the discrepancy between exterior appearance
and interior reality that such playacting necessarily presupposes, and reassures his *privado* by telling him to disbelieve
royal anger unless he is ordered imprisoned (949b). The King's
words also make manifest the metaphysics that is at the heart
of this drama when he directs Enrique to ignore material
signifiers (*palabras*) and to see only his secret meaning and
essence (*alma*).

It is at this moment, however, that Ludovico re-enters unno-
ticed by the King and Enrique, and sees Alfonso raising his
privado up from the ground, thereby discovering that the
latter's fall is nothing more than a trap, a fiction (949b).
Ludovico therefore follows the King's example and becomes a
type of writer himself, when he attempts to turn the monarch's
deception back on him by accusing Enrique of treason. Thus
begins Alfonso's need to verify the loyalty of his own trusted
advisor. This is a process which does not bode well for the latter, for the King is now confronted with a series of signs that
appear to point unequivocally to Enrique's guilt. It is in this
sense that the primary plot, involving the conspiracy, parallels
the secondary amorous one: just as ostensible appearances lead
Enrique to jump to incorrect conclusions about Elena and
Porcia, so too do they lead the King to conclude mistakenly that
Enrique is guilty. The first of these ostensible signs is, of
course, Ludovico's and the princes' accusation that Enrique has
committed treason.

The second sign appears immediately after, when Elena tells

Alfonso that Enrique is maintaining a written correspondence with King Carlos VIII of France. Such a secret correspondence would, of course, constitute an explicit act of treason. Elena's information is based on another equally misleading sign: the signature of Carlos VIII which César had presented to her, thinking that it was a love note from Enrique. When César delivers it and sees Elena's reaction of shock and anger, he looks at the paper for the first time and, seeing the French king's signature, is unable to believe *appearances*:

> Dudando estoy y suspenso
> con lo que mis ojos ven.
> Pienso que Enrique es leal;
> la firma del francés veo:
> y así ni a los ojos creo
> ni al pensamiento . . .
>
> (951a)

Ser and *parecer* are directly contradictory; the only way César can explain what he sees is by conjecturing that there has been a mix-up: "aun en comedias me enfada / ver *dos papeles trocados*" (951a). In this gesture of self-reference, Tirso's play points to one of its own primary focuses: the dangers of writing. The closed and secretive nature of the written word, the fact that its content is "hidden" (as in the case of two pieces of paper which, folded, are often subject to being mistaken for one another) is one of the things that makes it potentially dangerous. But César's metadramatic commentary also implicitly emphasizes the other two *papeles* that will be switched in the same mistaken yet much more dangerous way: Enrique's fictional role as fallen favorite that was scripted by the King and his new role—scripted by Ludovico and the princes and progressively read by the King—as a traitor. Both forms of *papel*, "paper" and "role," serve equally well to conceal and to defer the truth of the matter.

Elena informs the King that César also knows of the illicit correspondence that is apparently taking place between Enrique and the French monarch. Unable to believe Elena's accusation, Alfonso asks César if Enrique is communicating with Carlos VIII. César responds affirmatively (953a), based on the signature he has seen, but before he can attempt to offer the explanation that he himself has conjectured (namely, that Enrique accidentally switched the note intended for Elena with the signature he had received from the conspirators), the King dismisses him. César's interrupted response therefore constitutes the third ostensible sign pointing to Enrique's guilt.

Unable to believe even these powerful signs, Alfonso finally appeals to Enrique himself. When Enrique, who believes that they are being watched by the conspirators, falsely admits his guilt and then realizes that Alfonso's anger is genuine, he bemoans the dangerous ambivalence to which he has fallen victim: "apenas / hay quien distinga y conozca / si lo que finge es de veras" (954a-b). The King is thereby deceived by what was originally his own fictive deception. Having believed this fourth apparent sign of Enrique's guilt (the *privado*'s own feigned confession), Alfonso immediately imprisons him.

When Porcia learns of Enrique's imprisonment, she appeals to the King's better judgment:

> Señor, a pedirte vengo,
> atrevida y pïadosa,
> que justifiques las culpas
> de Don Enrique, y conozcas
> que no es bien que tú te enojes,
> sin mirar que *la paloma*
> *al aire blanca parece,*
> *aunque sea negra toda.*
> *El agua clara en un vidrio,*
> *turbia a nuestro ser la tornan*
> *los rayos del sol hermoso;*
> *en las cristalinas ondas*
> *corvos parecen los remos:*
> muchos espejos nos borran,
> si en las cosas claras vemos
> que hay peligro, en las dudosas,
> ¿qué será, Rey poderoso?
>
> (954b-55a)

This passage explicitly reiterates what has become a familiar motif: the deceptive nature of appearances. With pairs of visual images, each of whose members is in direct opposition to the other, Porcia posits a *ser* that is radically opposed to *parecer*: *negra/blanca*; *clara/turbia*; [*rectos*]/*corvos*. The second term of these oppositions, that is, the unreal appearance, functions as a distorting visual *supplement* to the reality that lies hidden beneath it. Porcia summarizes by stating that if there is potential danger in what appears to be clear, then there surely must be in that which explicitly inspires doubt.[9]

When Alfonso observes the diametrically opposed treatment of Enrique by the two women, he is at a loss to explain it except as some form of deception: "¡La que le quiere, me avisa; / la que no le quiere, aboga / por Enrique! *Aquí hay engaño*" (955a). Enrique has not only mixed up the two papers (the French king's signature and the love note intended for Elena); he has similarly mixed up and mistaken the true nature of the two women, as we have seen. Porcia therefore implicitly yet innocently supplies Alfonso with a tangible example of the deceptive nature of appearances, precisely the point that she was trying to impress upon him.

Alfonso is finally convinced of Enrique's innocence when the *privado*, ordered to produce the French king's signature, shows instead the note that he had meant to send to Elena. The King thus becomes aware of his own misunderstanding, caused by a confusion of *papeles*, both "papers" and "roles." César further verifies Enrique's innocence by producing the signature. Alfonso has learned the potential danger of appearances, as Porcia had suggested. He summarizes ("Quien no apura ni acrisola / la verdad, errores hace") and immediately orders the death of the conspirators (956a).

Enrique advises, however, that Alfonso must not take public responsibility for bringing these powerful conspirators to justice if he wishes to avoid reprisals by their families and supporters. The King therefore devises a final *cautela* that will enable him to do just that: by way of a written note, he secretly orders the Prince of Taranto to go with his men to a certain plaza where Enrique will be in costume (in celebration of *Carnestolendas*), but may be identified by a white cloth that he will take out; the Prince is to take out a similar white cloth and then to kill him. Alfonso proceeds secretly to give identical written orders to the Prince of Salerno. The two princes carry out their orders, and—each believing he is killing Enrique—unknowingly kill one another.

Now, there is no dramatically necessary reason for the King to communicate his orders to the princes in writing. The fact that he does so serves, however, to continue and to complete a motif that is consistent throughout: when the stage directions tell us that Alfonso sits down to write two *papeles* (956a), the term has all of the significance that *Cautela*'s entire action has cumulatively conferred upon it until this point. Alfonso is, in effect, scripting new roles for the two princes. Each prince is, from his own point of view, enacting the role of executioner of Enrique that the King has apparently assigned him. But neither realizes that the role of Enrique is, in fact, being played by the other prince. The King's final written notes conform to the pattern that is so central to the entire drama: they *appear* to order Enrique's death but in fact function to bring about a result that is directly opposed to it, the princes' deaths and Enrique's social "resurrection." The potential ambivalence and reversibility of the written *supplement* is thereby enacted.

The costumes worn in celebration of Carnival enable Alfonso's final *cautela* to function effectively. Because of them, the princes are dependent on the King's directions that lead them to read deceptive exterior signs (the *lienzos*) to identify their would-be victim. Carnival is indeed an appropriate context for *Cautela*'s action, for disguise, absence, and hidden reality are prevalent throughout. It is appropriate in other senses as well. Carnival is inevitably associated with carnality, that is, the pleasures of the flesh: sexuality, ritualized violence, and the conspicuous consumption of food, particularly meat, from which the name derives (Peter Burke ch. 7). It occurs just prior, and is clearly opposed, to Lent, a time of relative spirituality during which the consumption of meat is prohibited.

The opposition of carnality and spirituality is utilized by Frank Kermode in his study of the Gospels, *The Genesis of Secrecy*, to distinguish between two types of interpretation. A "carnal" reading of a text, he tells us, denotes an immediate, superficial, sensorial comprehension, while a "spiritual" reading denotes a deeper, more profound one: "There is seeing and hearing, which are what naive listeners and readers do; and there is perceiving and understanding, which are in principle reserved to an elect" (3). Kermode's distinction nicely illustrates the opposition of exterior appearance and hidden reality that is at the heart of *Cautela contra cautela*: apparent signifiers (*carne*) are deceptive and confusing to those who do not know how to read the reality (*espíritu*) that they simultaneously hide and disclose. Carnival therefore serves a symbolic function in *Cautela*, for both plots constitute an extended trope, a ritualized and carnivalesque masquerade by which society, as represented by Alfonso's reign in Naples, is prepared for its "Lent": presumably, a more peaceful, more spiritual reign, in which transcendent values may hold sway without the necessarily corrupting influence of exterior and "supplemental" carnal signifiers, such as the written word. *Cautela*'s metaphysics, as we have seen, constitutes a consistent denigration of the material signifier.

The carnival motif is therefore most fitting: *Cautela contra cautela* and its various forms of metadrama revolve around the opposition of appearance and reality, of disguise and disclosure. These oppositions are intimately associated with the notion of *papeles*, both literal and figurative, that undermine conventional communicative processes and the social order on which these depend. It is also strangely fitting that the original author of the warnings to the King about the conspiracy remains unknown. This final and mysterious anonymity—an ambivalent, inscrutable authorship that gives origin to and hangs over the action of the entire drama—underlines the dangers of writing, an act that is inevitably marked by absence.

At the center of Tirso's *Cautela contra cautela* is a radical ideological opposition that is an important aspect of Baroque sensibility, as pointed out by Sullivan: that between interior transcendent spiritual values—the "true" reality of eternal existence—and their necessary subjugation to exterior, material expression—the "apparent" and transient reality of earthly existence.[10] This bodily exteriorization of spiritual essence constitutes a symbolic death—always associated in the metaphysical tradition with the written word—and parallels the Catholic doctrine whereby the Son of God takes on a necessarily human form and is subjected to crucifixion. This paradox is brought to a crisis by the forces of the Reformation, whose emphasis on individual, inner (and therefore potentially subversive) faith results in the Counter-Reformation's polemical insistence on formal, institutional modes of exteriorization of faith as a means of ethical and religious control. It is a paradox that reappears, as we shall see, with even greater insistence in Calderón's *La cisma de Inglaterra*.

Chapter Five

Calderón's *La cisma de Inglaterra* and the Ethics of Erasure

I

"Tocan chirimías y córrese una cortina; aparece el Rey Enrique durmiendo; delante, una mesa, con recado de escribir, y, a un lado, Ana Bolena. Y dice el Rey entre sueños . . ." (75). It is with these stage directions that Calderón's *La cisma de Inglaterra* (1627?) begins. They introduce what is perhaps the principal thematic axis around which much of this drama revolves: the opposition of presence and absence. The curtain that is drawn aside to reveal the sleeping King constitutes a presentation: a revelation of what was previously hidden. The opening of any drama is always a presentation in the sense that it inevitably makes present to the audience something that had previously been absent. In this respect, *La cisma*'s opening is highly ironic, for what is revealed is not a "presence," at least not in the usual sense of the term. It is rather an image of absence: a motionless stage, a presence deferred. This lack creates an expectation of action, especially with the regal sound of the *chirimías*. We have been prepared for an entrance because, as a literary genre, drama predicates the notions of presence and action; but the opening scene thoroughly defeats this expectation. The King does *not* majestically appear, strutting onstage with royal bearing, in active fashion. Rather, he is revealed: in effect, Enrique is absent by virtue of the fact that he is asleep. The sense of presence that is implied by conscious and intentional agency is therefore doubly deferred. Not only does the opening of the drama disappoint our primary expectations of intentional agency; when it *does* present such an agent, his presence is again deferred by his unconscious state.

This image of the sleeping King manifests another motif: the unconscious. The first scene is, in fact, the onstage representation of what Enrique is dreaming while he is asleep. The unconscious is implicitly related to absence, for it represents that which is not "present" to the conscious mind. At the same time, it implies the absence of the subject from self-consciousness and from the possibility of intentional acts.

The written word makes an immediate and explicit appearance in the stage directions ("delante, una mesa, con recado de escribir"). Writing's inherent connection with absence has already been established in earlier chapters of this study. The opposition between presence and absence is thus implicit in these opening stage directions and throughout the first scene, but always connected to and manifested by such motifs as sleep, the unconscious, and writing.

The drama's action begins with King Enrique VIII's dream about a brief encounter with an unknown woman. When Ana Bolena appears in court soon thereafter, Enrique identifies her as the woman of his dream and immediately conceives a passion for her. Now, the King's chief advisor, Cardinal Volseo, has a great ambition to power: in his youth, an astrologer had predicted that he would someday attain a high ranking, but that a certain woman would bring about his downfall. When Queen Catalina abruptly dismisses Volseo from court, he believes that she must be the woman referred to in the prophecy. He therefore promises Ana Bolena that he will eliminate Catalina and make *her* queen, on condition that he (Volseo) always remain in Ana's graces. The equally ambitious Ana readily agrees, despite her present romantic involvement with Carlos, the French ambassador. Knowing Enrique's desperate passion for Ana, Volseo advises him to divorce Catalina and marry Ana. Enrique follows this advice and publicly divorces Catalina, who refuses to accept the divorce but goes into exile. Enrique marries Ana in a secret ceremony. Exercising the power of her newly attained position, Ana immediately has her father, Tomás, made *presidente* of the realm. When Volseo complains to her that he had wanted the position himself and then threatens to remove her from power in the same way that he had removed Catalina, Ana immediately informs Enrique of Volseo's threats. The King strips Volseo of his office and properties and sends him into exile, where he (according to all indications) does away with himself. Enrique meanwhile learns of Ana's romantic involvement with Carlos; he disavows his love for her and immediately orders her execution. He now regrets his divorce from Catalina and decides to reinstate her as queen, only to learn that she has died. He therefore orders their daughter, Princess María, to take an oath of office as future Queen of England and orders the nobility to swear their loyalty to her. The drama ends with these oaths.

At first glance, the action of *La cisma de Inglaterra* appears to be a progression "from order disturbed to order restored," the structure established by Arnold G. Reichenberger as standard for the *comedia* (307). Clearly, the King's passion for Ana Bolena and his subsequent divorce from Catalina constitute a breaking of the social and religious order, an order that is provisionally restored when he ultimately repents and names María as future Queen of England. Although this description *does* do justice to the drama's basic structure, it is somewhat misleading: although the restoration of order *is* accomplished in the final scene, its duration is left open to question, the seeds of contention having been sown by the very act that appears to guarantee it.

Calderón's drama is organized around various oppositions according to which the principal characters are, themselves, defined and opposed. One such character opposition is between Ana Bolena and Catalina. Likewise, Cardinal Volseo is opposed to a relatively minor character, Tomás Boleno, in certain respects. The King, however, is the focal point of these character oppositions and of other more conceptual ones, such as presence/absence, consciousness/unconsciousness, public duty/private desires, interiority/exteriority, Catholicism/Protestantism, reason/passion, and free will/determinism. The next part of this chapter is devoted to examining some of these oppositions.

Like so many *comedias*, *La cisma* is self-consciously concerned with the processes and limits of communication: the ways in which communicative acts succeed or fail and how they attain or are given authority. It establishes a relation between certain acts of communication and the institutions upon which society bases itself. The third part of this chapter, therefore, focuses specifically on written communication in its various dimensions: reading, writing, re-reading, erasure, and rewriting.

II

The opposition of presence and absence pervades *La cisma de Inglaterra*. Any king implicitly embodies this opposition because, by virtue of his public function, he is—like the king in *El villano en su rincón*—institutionally, symbolically present in all the corners of the realm. The price of this public presence is, however, the essential deferral of his private self, an absentation of his individuality. This paradoxical embodiment of presence and absence is one of the central issues of *La cisma de Inglaterra*, for, like many of the dramas studied thus far, it too dramatizes the constant struggle between public capacity and private motive.

In the particular case of Enrique, the balance of presence and absence has been shifted almost completely in the direction of the latter: the unconscious absence that characterizes Enrique in the first scene is only the first of various forms of absence that characterize him throughout. Only near the very end of the drama does he awaken to certain aspects of the reality that now surrounds him and that he has rather unwittingly helped to create. The character who most contributes to the King's absence in this regard is Volseo. As cardinal and chief advisor to Enrique, Volseo habitually restricts the direct access of others to him, thereby absenting him from his full and effective functioning as a monarch. By maintaining the King in a state of relative isolation (and, thereby, of self-absorption and confusion), the Cardinal is enabled to manipulate him and to further his own ambitions.[1]

Volseo refuses, for example, to allow even Queen Catalina in to see her husband (647-71). Throughout the entire first half of the drama, he defers presenting Carlos, the French ambassador, to the King. Volseo knows that the message that Carlos bears—proposing the future marriage of the Princess María to a French prince—could threaten his own personal ambitions to the papacy. The Cardinal, in fact, utilizes the mutual absence of the French and Spanish kings—the geographic distance that separates them—and masterly plays them off against one another by promising separately and contradictorily that he will marry off María in a way that will be of political advantage to each. In this way, he procures the separate support of both of them in his own bid for the papal seat (1249-60). Needless to say, he has also secretly absented the King by usurping his right and duty to arrange the marriage of his only daughter and legitimate heir. The irony arising from Enrique's relation to the dichotomy of presence and absence is, of course, that as king he is the one figure who should be most "present," precisely in terms of such civic affairs as these.

It is this pervasive and insidious use of absence that best characterizes Volseo. Its most telling effects are, of course, where Enrique is concerned, for while Volseo has an active and pragmatic relationship with absence (he uses it), the King is, for the most part, its passive victim (it uses him). In effect, Volseo helps to create and maintain a process whereby Enrique is consistently absented from the presence of others and made to believe that his life as a private individual takes precedence over his institutional role as king. (The object of Enrique's private motivation is Ana Bolena, who is likewise driven by purely selfish motives; by way of contrast, Queen Catalina embodies the motif of unselfishness.) The inevitable result of the progressive absence that Volseo exploits is a subversion of the very system that sustains such institutions as the monarchy.

It is only near the end of the drama that the King utilizes absence, or what amounts to hidden presence, when he listens from behind a curtain to what people are saying about him around the palace (2552-61). It is by way of this duplicity that Enrique finally discovers Ana's own duplicity and unfaithfulness. He who was asleep behind a curtain at the beginning of the drama (see opening stage directions, quoted above), is somewhat more awake by the drama's end, although still behind a curtain, still deferred.

The opposition of presence and absence is also implied by the drama's title: the notion of *cisma* is one of disjunction or separation, a present division that betokens a former unity. *Autoridades*'s definition of *cisma* begins: "División, discordia, separación de los miembros de un cuerpo místico de su cabeza. . . ." The term *cisma* represents a type of absence: a conscious exclusion, the "trace" of a presence that was, but that no longer is. The title therefore does not refer only to the schism that exists between England and the Roman Catholic Church by the end of the drama, a schism that Enrique has established in order to divorce Catalina legally and marry Ana Bolena. It also refers to the ethical and communicative universe—the "moral" schism—of a universe that is pervaded by an essential absence and darkened by the deferral, the ultimate unknowability, of others' or even of one's own self.

Another opposition that is related to that of presence and absence is interiority/exteriority: the ways in which surface appearances or outer, public signs have the function of hiding or disguising an inner, private reality that is very different from or even opposed to them. This type of deception, this absenting of self, is practiced primarily by Ana and Volseo (Bacigalupo 215-16). Ana's duplicity in this sense is most emphasized by frequent references to her physical beauty. Her father Tomás, her lover Carlos, and Enrique consistently refer to Ana's charms, but their descriptions are inevitably offset by misgivings about her inner motives and impulses. Near the beginning of Act I, for example, when Tomás requests that Carlos accompany him in welcoming his daughter to court, he describes Ana's extreme beauty:

> . . . tengo una hija, corona
> de cuantas bellezas dio
> al mundo Naturaleza,
> pues a su rara belleza
> otra ninguna igualó.
>
> (280-84)

The "crown" that Tomás invokes serves both to symbolize Ana's physical (exterior) beauty and to anticipate her hidden (interior) agenda: the acquisition of power by way of the Crown.

Soon thereafter, when Ana shows herself to be ungrateful to her father for his help and scornfully rejects his advice concerning how she should conduct herself in court, Tomás responds: "Siempre de tu condición, / por los discursos crueles, / temí lastimosos fines" (743-45). Carlos, too, recognizes that Ana's physical beauty hides a morally "ugly" interior. After hyperbolically praising her beauty, he expresses misgivings about her character and proceeds to make explicit Ana's tendency to use false appearances to hide her inner nature:

Su vanidad, su ambición,
su arrogancia y presunción
la hacen, a veces, esquiva,
arrogante, loca y vana;
y aunque en público la ves
católica, pienso que es
en secreto luterana.

(450-56)[2]

When the King sees Ana for the first time, he seems to recognize her as the woman who had appeared in his dream:

¿Quién eres? ¿Cómo te nombras,   [*A Ana.*]
mujer, que deidad pareces
y con beldad me enterneces,
si con agüeros me asombras?
Entre luces, entre sombras
causas gusto y das horror;
entre piedad y rigor
me enamoras y me espantas;
y, al fin, entre dichas tantas
te tengo miedo y amor.

(859-68; emphasis in original)

A sense of irony arises from the discrepancy between Ana's "divine" appearance ("que deidad pareces") and her secret motivations, which are anything but divine. The opposition between appearance and underlying, deferred, "absented" reality is emphasized by the consistently contrary feelings and images that she inspires in Enrique: *luces/sombras*; *gusto/horror*; *piedad/rigor*; *enamoras/espantas*; *miedo/amor*.

An obvious example of the way Ana intentionally cultivates outward appearances in order to further her ambitions is the great display of humility with which she greets Queen Catalina upon entering the palace for the first time. This ostensible humility is in direct contrast to her actual feelings of pride and jealousy (493-512) (Fischer 120). When Ana first meets Enrique, she disguises her envy and her ambition in much the same way that she had earlier with Catalina, that is, with a great show of courtesy and humility. In this second case, however, her utter duplicity is highlighted in dramatic fashion by an aside; when she bows down to show her humility, Enrique offers to pick her up in his arms and Ana responds:

> Si en tus brazos me levantas,
> tocaré las luces santas
> del sol; mas no será bien
> que vuele más alto quien
> está, señor, a tus plantas.
> En ellas vivo dichosa
> y en ellas . . . (¡rabiando muero!)   *Aparte*.
> mayor esfera no quiero.
>
>   (884-91; emphasis in original)

Enrique describes Ana as "divina y bella" (904) when he exits, yet Ana's "divinity" is uniformly related to her physical beauty, which serves to mask her true motives.

Ana's pattern of deception continues throughout the drama. In Act II, when Volseo approaches her and tells her to feign love for the King, she speaks of her own ability to deceive:

> . . . pedir
> que sólo sepa fingir,
> sabiendo que soy mujer
> y que soy Bolena yo,
> bien excusarse pudiera;
> pues por ser mujer fingiera,
> cuando por Bolena no.
>
>   (1390-96)

When the King declares his love to Ana (1559-61), she excuses herself, according to the plan that Volseo and she have agreed upon, by invoking her sense of honor:

> Procuras
> tú mi deshonra clara;
> que el ser tu esposa ya me disculpara;
> pero no el ser tu dama.
> Y, así, piedad no esperes.
> Si me estimas y quieres,
> no borres hoy la fama
> que limpia y clara vive.
>
>   (1572-79)

These forceful lines indicate a rather devious use of the honor code, whose most common manifestation is the reputation or *fama* that a given individual enjoys in society at large. *Fama* normally serves as the publicly "legible," outer sign of an individual's personal worth and integrity. But in this example it is explicitly reduced by Ana's words to pure social appearance: an empty and misleading signifier whose purpose is none other than to disguise its opposite, the dishonor of which she will prove all too capable. Paradoxically, Ana uses the honor code to dishonor Enrique. In this sense, her pattern of linguistic and social disruption is similar to King Sancho's in *La estrella de Sevilla*. We have seen such discrepancy or disjunction manifest itself in different variations not only in *La estrella*, but also in *El ejemplo mayor de la desdicha* and most obviously in *Cautela contra cautela*.

Much of Volseo's characterization develops according to the same pattern of duplicitous discrepancy between outer (present) appearances and inner (absent) reality. Perhaps the most obvious example of this occurs when he refuses to allow Catalina to enter the King's quarters, near the end of Act I, and she reacts angrily:

> ¡Loco, necio, vano!
> Por Príncipe soberano
> de la Iglesia hoy os respeto;
> aquesa púrpura santa
> que, por falso y lisonjero,
> de hijo de un carnicero
> a los Cielos os levanta,
> me turba, admira y espanta. . . .
>
> (660-67)

Catalina recognizes that beneath the robes he wears in his official function as cardinal ("aquesa púrpura santa") are interior selfish motives that are radically opposed to the Christian ethic that those robes and that office ostensibly represent. This discrepancy is even more ironic, given Volseo's ambition to ascend to the papacy.

Volseo indoctrinates the King into this process of deception. He first advises Enrique to hide his true feelings from Ana (869) and later convinces him to justify publicly his divorce from

Catalina with false arguments and what we would call, simply, a "good acting job":

> Llama tu Parlamento,
> y, junto, haz un retórico argumento
> diciendo que te aflige la conciencia
> a tomar contra el Papa esta licencia;
> y, mostrando que es celo aqueste intento,
> haz extremos, señor, de sentimiento.
>
> (1697-1702)

Following this advice, Enrique does indeed annul his marriage to Catalina by claiming, most insincerely, that it is a way of defending the Faith. Near the end of the drama Enrique says that he will pretend to be in merry spirits in order to procure the good will of the royal council: "Quiero prevenirme / a disimularme afable, / a consolado fingirme" (2851-53). These examples of duplicity are similar to Ana's and Volseo's: Enrique's words and gestures directly contradict and disguise an inner, subversive truth. Presence, in the sense of the expression of true feelings and motivations, is inevitably deferred.

An opposition that is related to interiority and exteriority, and that is in fact a variation of it, is private motivations versus civic responsibilities. Volseo and, later on, the King consistently subordinate public duty to personal desires. The Cardinal views his office as nothing more than a means of furthering his personal ambitions. He literally *uses* his official position—along with the institutional codes of both the Church and courtly society that sustain and define it—to further himself. He has, for example, deferred the meeting between Enrique and the French ambassador, in spite of the fact that this goes "Contra las humanas leyes" (1249).

Knowing Enrique's lust for Ana, the Cardinal promises to procure her for him in return for support in his bid to become Pope, a condition to which Enrique readily agrees. In effect, Volseo and the King "sell" themselves to one another. A similar transaction occurs between Volseo and Ana when they agree to help one another in realizing personal ambitions, regardless of the consequences for the kingdom. When Volseo later

convinces the King to divorce Catalina and to marry Ana, he
justifies this plan by the principle that a monarch's personal life
takes precedence over his institutional functioning as ruler:

> Más importa la vida
> de un Rey que ver perdida
> la Majestad que os mide
> cetro y laureles de oro.
>
> (1642-45)

While invoking the age-old institutional symbols of monarchy,
such as the *cetro* and the *laureles*, Volseo simultaneously denies them by claiming that they are worthless unless the ruler
who wears them enjoys a sense of personal fulfillment. This
directly contradicts the notion (see above, p. 118) that effective monarchy is made possible precisely by the forfeiture, the
absenting, of a king's personal, individual existence. When
Enrique marries Ana shortly after divorcing Catalina (2102-11),
it is precisely the secrecy of the ceremony that is most ironic in
this context: the wedding of a king, normally the most public,
ceremonial, and communal of affairs is, in this case, paradoxically private in every sense of the word.

Catalina is well aware of Volseo's selfish motives. Early in
the action she dismisses him from court (1077-81). When
Enrique asks her why, the Queen is most blunt in her reply:

> Justas causas
> me mueven. Tengo a Volseo
> por lisonjero, y que entabla
> más su aumento que el provecho
> del reino; que sólo trata
> de subir al sol, midiendo
> la soberbia y la arrogancia.
>
> (1086-92)

Catalina sees Volseo as a dangerous abuser of official power.
The character most opposed to this type of abuse is Ana's father,
Tomás Boleno. As *presidente* of the kingdom, Tomás receives
the King's order to execute his own daughter near the end of
the drama, but swears that he will administer justice, regardless of personal motivations:

> Aunque pudiera
> como padre, en fin, rendirme
> a la pasión, no pretendo
> sino que el mundo publique
> que he sido juez, y no padre.
>
> (2695-99)

Nothing could be more contrary to Volseo's absolute selfishness than Tomás's strong sense of civic duty: his public role as judge takes precedence even over his relation with his daughter.

The question of civic duty comes up repeatedly. It is explicitly raised in the drama's final scene. Princess María is about to take her oath of office, when the *capitán* enumerates her responsibilities:

> Su Alteza
> ha de jurar cumplir
> su obligación, que es aquésta:
> que *ha de conservar en paz*
> *sus vasallos, aunque sea*
> *a costa de su descanso,*
> obligación de quien reina.
>
> (2891-97)

These words are, of course, in direct opposition to Volseo's earlier justification for Enrique's divorce from Catalina (1642-45) that gives precedence to the personal life of a king over his public one. The drama's opening scene anticipates the King's generally lax behavior with regard to his office: the first presentation of Enrique is, we remember, as a sleeping king. *Autoridades*'s second, more figurative definition of the verb *dormir* is interesting in this context: "Se toma por descuidarse uno en la obligación de su empleo, obrando con menos solicitud de la que se requiere." It is clearly this form of sleep that best characterizes Enrique's relation to his public office.

María, finally, is a character who stands with Catalina and Tomás on the side of civic duty. Her relation to this motif is complicated, however, by her allegiance to what she considers an even higher cause. One of the conditions by which the nobility will swear allegiance to her, in the drama's final scene, is that she promise not to re-establish official ties to the Pope. She refuses to agree to this condition, claiming to her father:

> ... pues Vuestra Majestad
> sabe la verdad, no quiera
> que, por razones de Estado,
> la ley de Dios se pervierta.
>
> (2922-25)

María insists on observing the law of God before any other law, be it civic or familial. Her insistence is most powerful in that it constitutes an implicit refusal to bow to Enrique's authority both as her king and as her father.

This last quotation is related to yet another opposition that complements those discussed thus far: Catholicism versus Lutheranism. Carlos, we remember, suspects Ana of secretly being a Lutheran (454-56). Her suspected Lutheranism is yet another hidden reality and is negatively contrasted with Catholicism, precisely by virtue of its secretive and therefore subversive nature. Volseo, Ana, and the King are all implicitly associated with the "negative" ideology of Luther by virtue of their very acts.

Conversely, Catalina and María are consistently portrayed as bearers of the standard of Catholicism. Catalina in particular embodies the virtues of "true" Christianity, i.e., Roman Catholicism. For example, when Ana meets the Queen for the first time, the courtly humility that she exhibits is so extreme that Catalina cannot help but characterize and chastise it as a form of heresy:

> De la tierra os levantad,
> que esas ceremonias son
> de quien con vana ambición
> a lo divino se atreve,
> porque sólo a Dios se debe
> tan debida adoración.
>
> (517-22)

Aside from the celestial imagery that other characters, including the King, consistently use to describe Catalina, she reinforces this idea with her own words and deeds. Contrary to the selfish motives of Ana or Volseo, she expresses more concern about her husband's state of health and mind than about her own: "¡Vos sin salud, señor mío, / y yo viva! ¡Vos con causa / de tristeza y yo no muero!" (1039-41). She appears, in this way, to exemplify an altruism that borders on (Christian) self-sacrifice. Such altruism is, of course, directly related to public duty. When Enrique divorces her, Catalina refuses to enter a convent because she claims that she is still married, according to Roman Catholic law (1983-86). Finally, she embodies the virtue of forgiveness when, after Volseo's downfall and in spite of all the ill that he has brought down upon her, Catalina gives him her only possession, a chain she has just received as a gift: "La vida y alma te diera / por consolarte, Volseo" (2494-95).

Princess María's resolute faith becomes explicit in the final scene, when Enrique attempts to convince her to follow the course of political expediency by agreeing to the condition that the nobles have attached to their oath of loyalty. She, however, refuses:

> INFANTA: Lo que importa es que a la Iglesia
> humildes obedezcamos;
> y yo, postrada por tierra,
> la obedezco, renunciando
> cuantas humanas promesas
> me ofrezcan, si ha de costarme
> negar la ley verdadera.
> REY: No se niega aquí la ley;
> algunos preceptos de ella,
> sí.
> INFANTA: Pues quien en uno falta,
> a todos los hace ofensa.
>
> (2947-57)

Her refusal is, of course, an implied indictment of Enrique's whole pattern of behavior, for he has—from her point of view—blatantly transgressed many of the precepts of "la ley verdadera."

Enrique is presented at the outset of the drama as absent and passive; "passivity" is, of course, etymologically related to passion. (Both derive from Latin *patior*, "to bear, support, undergo, suffer, endure" [Lewis]). The image of the sleeping King is the first of a series of references that characterize Enrique as being led more by passion than by reason. This passion is embodied by Ana, who ultimately inspires him to abandon his marriage with Catalina. At the beginning of Act II, when Volseo sees Enrique's agitated state, he tells him to relax, but the King responds that he cannot:

> Mal podré,
> que quien sin discurso ama,
> sólo en sus penas sosiega,
> sólo en su llanto descansa.
>
> (909-12)

The oppositions *penas/sosiega* and *llanto/descansa* express the King's confused state of mind: he can take solace only in that which gives him pain. Such paradoxes are, of course, part of the standard rhetorical apparatus of courtly love, whose self-contradictory essence is often expressed by way of oxymora. Equally important is the fact that Enrique loves "sin discurso": we shall see that Enrique is "sin discurso" (literally, "without speech") throughout *La cisma*, in the sense that so many of his verbal acts are rendered void. But *discurso*'s other meaning is also at play here, for, as Francisco Ruiz Ramón acutely points out in his edition of *La cisma* (114n910), the term *discurso* "se toma muchas veces por el uso de la razón" (*Autoridades*). Enrique will use the term once again—and in very much the same sense—near the end of the drama, just after ordering Ana's execution: "Ay *discurso*, / ¿qué me atormentas y afliges?" (2738-39). He recognizes early on that he is driven by forces that appear to be more powerful than he or his kingship: ". . . las pasiones del alma, / ni las gobierna el poder, / ni la Majestad las manda" (930-32). Volsco later characterizes the King's love for Ana as implacable: "no hay respeto ni interés / a que se rinda su amor" (1376-77).

An interesting aspect of both these quotations is the lack of direct agency on the part of Enrique himself: it is not Enrique who, all things being proper, "governs" or "commands" the "passions of his soul." It is, rather, *poder* and *Majestad* that take on these functions and that are rendered significantly helpless. In the second quote, it is his *amor*, not Enrique himself, that will not obey any *respeto* or *interés*. This metonymic displacement—wherein a part or aspect of Enrique takes over a function that is most properly his—serves to underline much of the drama's more explicit characterization of him. This special use of metonymy represents the same deferral and absentation of self that we have seen all along in regard to Enrique; in this case, it is manifested implicitly on the level of language itself.

The question of passion versus reason implies another, more theologically based opposition: free will versus determinism.

(This opposition appears, of course, time and again as a central preoccupation of Calderón's drama; the most obvious example that comes to mind is *La vida es sueño*.) It is clear that Enrique exercises very little free will, particularly when it comes to Ana:

> Puesto que mi albedrío
> a quererte me fuerza,
> sin que mi amor se tuerza,
> ya no es libre ni es mío.
>
> (1421-24)

Aside from the same sort of metonymic displacement that we have just seen in reference to the King ("mi albedrío," "mi amor"), Enrique's words represent a most paradoxical notion of *albedrío*: his will, he claims, "forces" him to love Ana. But if this is true, he does not choose or act freely. Neither his *albedrío* nor his *amor* is truly his—in the sense of possession and mastery—any longer: the King's self appears to be even more absent, even more radically deferred in this case. In all of these examples, there is an explicit pattern of terms that negate themselves, that are "self-erasing": power that does not govern, majesty that does not command, free will that is not free. It is this form of self-erasure that essentially characterizes Enrique.

Volseo and Ana are also driven by the passion of a relentless ambition to power. Much like the King, Ana consistently defers responsibility for her own acts by invoking powers that appear to be greater than she, as when she breaks her earlier vows of eternal love to Carlos:

> Carlos, perdona
> si tu firme amor ofendo
> cuando hoy aspirar pretendo
> al lustre de una corona.
> Mujer he sido en dejar
> que me venza el interés;
> séalo en mudar después,
> y séalo en olvidar.
> Que cuando lleguen a ver
> que el interés me ha vencido,
> que he olvidado y he fingido,
> todo cabe en ser mujer.
>
> (1397-1408)

Ana ascribes her own acts of treachery, not to free choice, but to her inherent nature as a woman; she claims that her actions were predetermined. Both she and the King embody that thoroughgoing determinism which has, from an orthodox Catholic point of view, often been associated with Lutheran thought.[3]

Catalina, María, and Tomás, on the other hand, embody the contrary Catholic doctrine of free will and consequent moral responsibility. As earlier noted, Tomás promises—near the end of the drama—to carry out the King's order to execute Ana, despite the fact that she is his daughter:

> ... no pretendo
> sino que el mundo publique
> que he sido juez, y no padre.
> Libre estoy, quedaré libre.
>
> (2697-2700)

Explicitly contrary to the King and others who are impelled by seemingly uncontrollable passions, Tomás takes full responsibility for his acts and performs his civic duty. He can do so because he is, in this sense, "free."

The problem of freedom and determinism raises the question of prophecy, which plays a central role in *La cisma*. A consideration of a minor character, Pasquín, is therefore in order, for he is one of those *graciosos* whose words—in the form of jokes, parables, and prophecies—turn out to be true, either literally or figuratively. Pasquín responds to the Queen's chastising of his *locuras* with a parable about a blind man (573-92) who lights his way in the darkness, not so that he may see, but so that others may see him. He proceeds to make an explicit analogy between the blind man of the story and himself: "yo con mis locuras / soy ciego y alumbro a oscuras" (600-01). The parable is in fact a figurative representation of the dark and morally blinded atmosphere of *La cisma* as a whole; the analogy that Pasquín makes is accurate, for his role within the court is precisely that of shedding light upon the truth, although that light may come in the form of dubious witticisms.[4] Indeed, Pasquín's status as court jester preconditions all responses to his various pronouncements and blinds those around him to the truth that they represent.

The parable of the philosopher and the soldier (938-66) that he tells Enrique serves to point up the all-too-human weaknesses and limitations to which Enrique himself is—most obviously—subject, notwithstanding his office. Discussing Pasquín's dramatic function, Ruiz Ramón notes:

> Su intervención invita a enfocar la atención del espectador en dos temas concretos, dramáticamente relacionados entre sí: los límites de la condición humana personificados en la Realeza y . . . la Corte, como el espacio de la apariencia. El primer tema, mediante el *exemplum* clásico del filósofo y el emperador Alejandro, incapaz con todo su poder de crear una humilde flor, pone de manifiesto la incapacidad del Rey como Rey para dominar sus pasiones . . . (Introduction 27)

Again, the conflict between private passions and public function is the central issue here. In recompense for these parables, the King grants Pasquín's request that he be made the court *figurín* or "denunciador de figuras" (979-87). In this capacity, he is to spot and denounce all falsity or pretense.

But Pasquín's most interesting role is that of "prophet," as he is first characterized by Carlos's servant: "siempre anda adivinando" (481). Meeting Ana Bolena for the first time, he declares that she has the face of a "gran bellaca" (615-16),[5] and goes on to predict:

> . . . seréis muy amada,
> muy querida y respetada;
> tanto, que ya os considero
> con aplauso lisonjero
> subir, merecer, privar,
> hasta poderos alzar
> con todo el imperio inglés,
> viniendo a morir después
> en el más alto lugar.
>
> (624-32)

Like his other commentaries that represent figurative truths, Pasquín's prophecies are inevitably realized. At the beginning of Act III, he predicts a humble, rather than a grandiose, burial for Volseo (2155-61). The central paradox concerning Pasquín is that, despite the truth of his words, he is—again, like

Aeschylus's Cassandra—destined never to be believed or taken seriously. Ruiz Ramón notes the great contrast between Pasquín's outward appearance (when he first enters, he is "vestido ridículamente") and the truth-value of what he says:

> . . . esa primera connotación de ridículo . . . contrasta drásticamente con la seriedad, la gravedad y la trascendencia de sentido que Pasquín aporta al universo dramático configurado por el resto de sus intervenciones. Su rasgo distintivo como personaje teatral es precisamente esa contradicción o, a lo menos, ese contraste entre su apariencia . . . y su función dramática . . . (Introduction 19)

This contrast obviously re-emphasizes the oppositions between interiority and exteriority, between appearances and reality.

The question of prophecy is, of course, related to that of predestination. Ana Bolena rationalizes her acts by appealing to deterministic forces such as her family background or her inherent nature as a woman (1390-1408). Volseo, for his part, believes in predestination as dictated by the stars. His absolute faith in a prophecy that he would someday attain great power has guided his every move. These concepts of determinism and predestination (that leave little room for free will) are, of course, directly contrary to the tenets of Roman Catholicism. It is precisely this direct association of Ana and Volseo with such justifications that so negatively characterizes them in the larger context of the drama as a whole.

Much like Ana, Enrique justifies his acts by ascribing them to forces he feels to be greater than his will: his passions. But he is also like Volseo in his belief in the power of Fate, as *written* in the stars, to determine human action. He thus laments his own betrayal of Catalina: "Esta fue mi desdicha, ésta mi estrella" (1771). Such justifications are dubious from an orthodox Roman Catholic standpoint because they serve to defer moral responsibility by way of absence. That is, they place human agency—always an act of essential presence—in the hands of either a predetermining force, such as inherent nature or family background (as in the case of Ana) or in those of an implacable future destiny that is prescribed by the stars (as in the case of Volseo). These explicit disavowals of free will and moral responsibility serve very well to exemplify the consistently negative characterization of Lutheranism that appears in *La cisma* (Loftis, "Henry VIII" 216). The justifications offered by Ana, Volseo, and the King effectively "absent" the morally integral subject. The drama implicitly sustains the argument for free will by repeatedly emphasizing these characters' ill-founded belief in such rationalizations. In effect, the drama tells us, such characters as Ana and Volseo have led their lives and built their identities upon such justifications; they have *freely* come to believe in them and thereby unwittingly created the conditions and circumstances that bring about their own downfalls. In this way they perfectly exemplify, not the power of predetermining forces nor that of predestining Fate; they illustrate, rather, the power of discourse itself to determine and affect human motives and actions: the self-fulfilling prophecy.

Prophecies are only one example of the many ways that language is both used and abused in *La cisma*. A brief consideration of some of its speech acts is therefore necessary.[6] Near the beginning of Act I, Enrique orders the kingdom to swear allegiance to his daughter María and names her as his sole legitimate heir (57-64). He later implicitly reverses this command when he banishes her from the court so that she may go live with her exiled mother (2248-50; 2518-21). He will ultimately void that banishment when he names her as princess and legitimate heir once again at the end of the drama (2802-04). This is only one example of how Enrique renders void his own declaratives by later contradicting them with others. As Ruiz Ramón has observed with reference to Enrique in his introduction: "Todas las acciones emprendidas por él o por él autorizadas llevan en sí mismas el principio y la semilla de su futura destrucción . . ." (51). This is most significant, for a king's functional role is largely based upon his institutional ability to issue and sustain public declaratives. In reference to Shakespeare's *Coriolanus*, Stanley Fish has observed that "declarative (and other) utterances do not merely mirror or reflect the state; they *are* the state, which increases and wanes as they are or are not taken seriously" (216). Enrique has therefore effectively absented himself from his public role as monarch on this linguistic level as well.

This is borne out near the end of Act II when Enrique publicly divorces and then banishes Catalina (1851-64). Aside from explicitly negating his own marriage vows, as well as the Pope's special dispensation which Enrique had personally requested and which had permitted the marriage to Catalina in the first place, he ends his speech in this way:

> . . . el vasallo que sintiere
> mal, advierta temeroso
> que le quitaré al instante
> la cabeza de los hombros.
>
> (1887-90)

Because Enrique knows that his argument for the divorce is a mere rationalization and that the divorce is therefore highly questionable, he feels obliged to back his words up with an explicit threat. This characterizes much of his linguistic behavior: by virtue of this continual "erasure" of his utterances—by his own personal conduct—he comes to feel that there is nothing to sustain him in his role of king except the threat of brute force. In speech act terms, we might say that the declaratives, directives, and commissives conventionally associated with the functional role of the monarch and that are an inherent part of that office are almost without exception made void in this drama because Enrique has in effect deferred his power and his office to those closest to him. Thus it is that both Volseo and Ana condition and recontextualize (thereby changing) the illocutionary force of so many of his utterances.

In *La cisma*, the fate of commissives—such as vows, oaths, and promises—depends almost entirely upon who utters them. Ana, Volseo, and Enrique do not honor with their actions the commissives they issue and often exploit such commissives to mask inner feelings and motives which run contrary to them. In effect, the *sincerity condition* deemed by Searle to be one of the prerequisites to the *happiness* of a commissive (*Speech Acts* 60) is consistently absent. When, near the end of Act I, for example, Ana and Carlos exchange vows of eternal love and marriage (760-829), the result is pathetically ironic, for we have already had indications that neither vow will be honored. Carlos has admitted privately to his servant that he wants Ana as a lover, but not as a wife (457-60). Ana, in turn, ultimately betrays these vows of undying love in order to satisfy her lust for power. Ironically, she will achieve this ambition by invoking even false vows of love to the King.

Commissives issued by characters such as Ana and Volseo
are always conditional, that is, based upon someone's promising something in return. Ana's vow of eternal fidelity to Volseo
takes on irony in this sense, partly because she will ultimately
betray it and partly because Volseo—who does not trust ordi-
nary commissives, thus revealing his own linguistic cynicism—asks her to authorize her promise with an oath. She
immediately complies:

> ¡Plegue a Dios que cuando intente
> ofensa tuya (después
> que tenga el cetro a mis pies
> y la corona en mi frente),
> que el aplauso y el honor
> que tanta dicha concierta
> tristemente se convierta
> en pena, llanto y dolor;
> y por fin más lastimoso
> de lo que al Cielo le plugo,
> muera a manos de un verdugo
> en desgracia de mi esposo!
> Esto juro, esto prometo.
>
> (1349-61)

Ana attempts to give authority to her promise to Volseo by
invoking God. In this case, the fragile and tenuous relation between Ana's discourse and the "world" is made explicit by its
ultimately self-referential nature, the fact that it functions in a
never-ending regress: language authorizing language, a promise backed up by an oath.

Ana does, of course, ultimately betray Volseo. When she
causes his downfall, the Cardinal curses her with another invocation of God that partially repeats Ana's earlier oath:

> ¡Plegue a Dios, que pues ingrata
> mi infame muerte deseas,
> que como me veo te veas;
> muera así quien así mata.
> Y pues al Cielo le plugo
> darme fin tan lastimoso,
> a ti te mate tu esposo
> a las manos de un verdugo.
>
> (2370-77)

The Cardinal asks that Ana's earlier oath come true; he wishes to make her accountable for her words. He asks God to act, in short, with a kind of justice ("como me veo te veas; / muera así quien así mata") that his own acts have implicitly denied. Ana does indeed die at the hands of an executioner, as ordered by her husband. Interestingly, Volseo's formal appeal to God, similar to Ana's, is the closest that he (the would-be Pope) ever comes to anything even remotely resembling a religious act. Irony lies in the fact that it is utilized in order to enact vengeance rather than (Christian) forgiveness: his prayer is in fact a curse.

As opposed to characters like Ana and Volseo, others such as Catalina, María, and Tomás always uphold their commissives. There is, however, one interesting exception to this rule: in the drama's final scene, María utters an oath that is voided by the context in which it is produced and by the very intentions that lie behind it. This final oath has important implications for the drama as a whole which will be investigated in Part IV of this chapter.

We have already seen that all prophecies in *La cisma de Inglaterra* come true and therefore have an inherent dramatic irony, for they are inevitably either not heeded, as in the case of Pasquín, or they are badly interpreted or applied, as in the case of Volseo and the astrologer of his youth (Herbold 29). This represents an extension, on the linguistic level, of some of the oppositions thus far discussed. Those speech acts, such as prophecies and curses, that defer personal responsibility to the arbitrary forces of Fate or to Divine Grace are ultimately fulfilled, often with an ironic sense. The original prophecy that inspires Volseo's ambition to power, for example, is fulfilled so literally that its consequences are decidedly disastrous, rather than beneficial, for the Cardinal:

> Un astrólogo me dijo
> que al Rey sirviese; que, así,
> *tan alto lugar tendría,*
> *que excediese a mi deseo.*
>
> (227-30)

Volseo achieves so high a position that it does indeed "exceed his desire": it is precisely this that brings about his ultimate downfall.

On the other hand, those speech acts that most substantially represent human presence, intentionality, and consequent moral responsibility are very often undermined. All these uses and misuses of language serve as constant reminders of the fragile and contingent quality of communication as it is practiced in the "Inglaterra" of Calderón's drama.

III

The written word is one of *La cisma*'s principal motifs. As noted earlier, the inclusion of a writing desk in the first scene immediately establishes an explicit relation between the King and the idea of inscription. This first scene establishes a pattern of "textual" imagery that is developed throughout. When Enrique sees the unidentified woman in his dream, he addresses her with the lines that open the drama:

> Tente, sombra divina, imagen bella,
> sol eclipsado, deslucida estrella.
> Mira que al sol ofendes
> cuando borrar tanto esplendor pretendes.
>
> (1-4)

He characterizes the unknown woman with a series of images of darkness: "*sombra* divina," "sol *eclipsado*," "*deslucida* estrella." This woman is, in effect, the manifestation of Enrique's "darker" irrational side: his unconscious sexual drives. The explicitly oppositional imagery of these opening verses helps to characterize the King, who himself embodies contrary motives: he has desires, but fears the object of those desires and what they might imply for his conscious, rational (and institutional) self. He therefore opposes the unknown woman's darkness by referring to himself symbolically as the sun. As monarch, he is the source of the kingdom's "light": its justice, reason, and honor. Enrique employs the imagery of writing—specifically, that of erasure—to express the idea that this woman actively opposes his role as *rey/sol*. But this sense of opposition is not solely between the King and the unknown woman of his dream. The imagery with which Enrique addresses her is self-contradictory: *luz*—not *sombra*—is conventionally associated with "divinity"; *sol* and *estrella*, both sources of light, are *eclipsado* and *deslucida*, respectively. *Imagen* has a somewhat negative connotation because it implies mere appearance, but is also positive in that it is *bella*. Enrique's use of erasure in a figurative sense (*borrar*) is significant, for it makes explicit the essence of his prior imagery: self-contradiction, a form of "self-erasure." Interestingly, it is precisely those values the King claims to embody (justice, reason, and honor) that will suffer the most radical erasure as the drama unfolds.

The idea of erasure is immediately made literal by the unknown woman, who responds to the King's protests by saying that she must erase whatever he writes (6). Her response takes on significance in relation to Lope's *El villano en su rincón*. In that drama, the King's act of writing serves as a metaphor for the general notion of governing: the King institutionally imposes order by way of cultural inscriptions, texts (both literal and figurative) that he writes and that are disseminated throughout the kingdom. Reading, its counterpart, represents those acts which the kingdom at large performs in response to those cultural inscriptions. If in *La cisma de Inglaterra*—as in *El villano*—the King's role is that of official "writer" for the kingdom, the implications of the unidentified woman's response are clear: her threatened erasure of Enrique's writings is the metaphorical equivalent of negating or canceling out his effective functioning as king. It is in this sense that her words provide an effective anticipation of much of the drama's action, for such erasure is consistent throughout.

The King's dream may be considered a type of unconscious writing. His sleeping state allows his unconscious to produce a text, a fleeting verbal exchange with an unknown woman. Because this writing was unconscious, Enrique, once he is awake, must read and interpret the text that he has created. He is an unconscious author who, as critic of his own work, must now find a pattern of conscious intelligibility. Enrique has already given evidence of "literary" inclinations: from the very beginning of the drama, he tends to experience events and to express himself by way of figurative language. We saw, for example, how he immediately portrayed himself metaphorically as the "sun" of the realm, its source of light, in opposition to the "darkness" of the unknown woman.

The next scene also emphasizes Enrique's role as reader and writer, this time, of books. Now that he need no longer fight militarily to defend the "true" Faith, that is, Roman Catholicism, he does so by means of his writings:

> ... ahora que Marte duerme
> sobre las armas sangrientas,
> velo yo sobre los libros,
> escribiendo en la defensa
> de los siete sacramentos
> aquéste con que hoy intenta
> mi deseo confundir
> los errores y las sectas
> que Lutero ha derramado;
> pues en él, para su ofensa,
> todo es refutar errores
> de un libro que se interpreta
> *Captividad Babilonia,*
> que es veneno, es peste fiera
> de los hombres.
>
> (77-91; emphasis in original)

As a defender of the Faith, Enrique is writing his book in order to combat the doctrines and influence of Martin Luther. This mention of Luther, of course, brings to the foreground a whole thematics that is insistently developed by the later action of the drama. The dialectic of such oppositions as Lutheranism/ Catholicism, determinism / free will, and private desires / public responsibility is, as we have seen, essential to the structure of *La cisma.*

The King proceeds to recount his dream to Volseo (91-116). He reveals that it was while working on his book concerning the seven sacraments that he had fallen asleep. This renders ironic his earlier statement that he was standing vigil over England's faith by means of books: "velo yo sobre los libros" (79). The implications of the King giving himself up to the forces of a "pesado sueño" while writing specifically about the sacrament of marriage are blatant enough in the context of the drama's later action. Upon falling asleep, claims Enrique, he saw a strange woman who approached him. The vision of this woman so disturbed him that he was no longer able to control his ability to write:

> Esta llegó a mí; y, turbado
> de considerarla y verla,
> ya no acertaba a escribir;
> pues cuanto con la derecha

mano escribía y notaba,
iba borrando la izquierda.

(111-16)

The King has apparently rewritten his dream/text. In the original dream, we remember, the unknown woman had threatened to erase all that Enrique wrote. In this retelling, it is his own left hand that now performs this action. The King thus incorporates and takes over the woman's function of erasure from the dream, transforming it into a part of himself. In so doing, he has made of himself a precarious union of motifs that tend to be contrary: his public duties as functioning monarch, represented by the right hand that does the writing, and his private, unconscious, and irrational desires, represented by his left, erasing hand. This is a continuation of the earlier pattern of imagery, invoked by Enrique throughout the drama, that combines contraries and that serves to illustrate his essentially confused and indecisive state of mind.[7] The inevitable result of such confusion on the part of the King is, to extend the writing metaphor, a blank page or a type of palimpsest: plainly put, a vacillating and uncertain reign.

Justification for this interpretation may be found in reference to both Freudian and Jungian thought. In "Freud and the Scene of Writing" (*Writing* 196-231), Derrida refers to Freud's use of the image of the "magic writing pad"—a children's toy which erases yet maintains the traces of past inscriptions—to describe the functioning of the psyche and, in particular, of the unconscious mind. The image of the "mystic writing pad"—as Derrida refers to it—seems quite appropriate to these opening scenes of *La cisma* (cf. Paul Julian Smith 133-34). Similarly, one cannot read this scene without thinking of the Jungian opposition between right and left: the right side is (arche-)typically thought of as having essentially positive attributes—such as rationality and consciousness—and the left side as having the corresponding negative attributes (Jung xvi, 211).

This valorized opposition between right and left goes back at least as far as Plato's *Phaedrus*, in which Socrates distinguishes between two types of love:

> . . . just as in a single physical body there are pairs of organs with the same name but distinguished as left and right respectively, so in our two speeches: both postulated madness

141

as a single generic form existing in us, but the first separated the left-hand part, as it were, and broke it down into further parts and did not give up till it detected among them what may be called a left-hand kind of love, which it very properly reprobated; whereas the second directed our attention to the types of madness on the right-hand side, and, finding there a kind of love which has the same name as the other but is divine, held it up before our eyes and eulogized it as the source of the greatest blessings that can fall to our lot. (82)

Another valorized opposition that is obviously related to this one appears near the end of the *Phaedrus*, when Socrates and Phaedrus distinguish between "good" (oral) communication and "bad" (written) communication:

> SOCRATES: Now can we distinguish another kind of communication which is the legitimate brother of written speech, and see how it comes into being and how much better and more effective it is?
> PHAEDRUS: What kind do you mean and how does it come about?
> SOCRATES: I mean the kind that is written on the soul of the hearer together with understanding; that knows how to defend itself, and can distinguish between those it should address and those in whose presence it should be silent.
> PHAEDRUS: You mean the living and animate speech of a man with knowledge, of which written speech might fairly be called a shadow. (98)

Jacques Derrida has translated this opposition to the realm of grammatology:

> There is . . . a good and a bad writing: the good and natural is the divine inscription in the heart and the soul; the perverse and artful is technique, exiled in the exteriority of the body. A modification well within the Platonic diagram: writing of the soul and of the body, writing of the interior and of the exterior, writing of conscience and of the passions . . . (*Grammatology* 17-18)

La cisma's King Enrique is caught between right-handed and left-handed impulses, between "good" writing (of his soul, his interior, and his conscience) and "bad" writing (of his body, his exterior, and his passions), between the writing that sustains the ethical imperatives of his kingdom and the erasure that threatens to subvert them. His essential confusion is the inevitable result of this situation. When he expresses the desire to "read" and interpret his dream, so as to understand its significance ("estoy despierto / considerando las señas" [119-20]), however, Volseo advises him to pay no attention to it:

> No haga la imaginación
> de esos discursos empeño;
> que las quimeras del sueño
> sombras y figuras son.
>
> (129-32)

The Cardinal attempts to divert Enrique even from his role as a reader of his own dream/text. He denies the necessity of giving any special attention to what the King has dreamed by explicitly associating it with examples of visual equivocation: *quimeras* and *sombras*.

Unlike *quimera* and *sombra*, however, the term *figura* has a wealth of connotations, rhetorical and otherwise, that make the interpretive act which it inspires an essential and inevitable part of what it is.[8] Like much of this drama's discourse, Volseo's argument is implicitly self-contradictory: he claims that one need not interpret that which by its very nature requires interpretation. Although he is ostensibly using the term *figura* here in one of its more common acceptances, that is, as a "representación o semejanza que se halla en alguna cosa, respecto de otra" (*Autoridades*), some of its other meanings are significant in the context of the drama as a whole. We have already seen, for example, that Pasquín has become the *figurín* or "denunciador de figuras" at court; thus it is that *figuras* are explicitly associated with the idea of deception or pretense. Related to this idea is the following definition of *figura*, also from *Autoridades*: "Se llaman los personajes que representan los Comediantes, fingiendo la persona del Rey, de la dama, y de otros diferentes estados." This definition brings to mind *La cisma*'s obvious metatheatrical aspect: the persistent role-playing, pretense, and deception in which nearly all of its characters indulge. The notion of *figura* is important in this sense because it well expresses that idea of deferral (of "truth," of "essential" self, of meaning) and the consequent need to "read" and interpret.

The motif of reading and writing continues soon thereafter, when Volseo delivers two letters to the King, one from Pope León X and the other from Martin Luther. Enrique immediately indulges his propensity to read things symbolically. These letters give him the means to make intelligible his earlier dream, which he can now reinterpret as their foreshadowing:

> Si fuera lícito dar
> al sueño interpretación,
> vieras que estas cartas son
> lo que acabo de soñar.
> La mano con que escribía
> era la derecha, y era
> la doctrina verdadera,
> que celoso defendía;
> aquesto, la carta muestra
> del Pontífice. Y querer
> deslucir y deshacer
> yo con la mano siniestra
> su luz, bien dice que lleno
> de confusiones vería
> juntos la noche y el día,
> la triaca y el veneno.
>
> (141-56)

Enrique identifies the letter from León X with the writing of true doctrine that he was doing with his own right hand and Luther's letter with the erasing action of his left. Within the apparent security of this new interpretation, he recognizes that his prior confusion was the result of the union within himself of contrary impulses that tended to neutralize or cancel one another out. This is here emphasized by the combining of such contraries as *noche/día* and *triaca/veneno*.

We have earlier heard mention of poison, when the King identified Martin Luther's book *Captividad Babilonia* with "veneno" (88-90). It is the *triaca/veneno* opposition that deserves some attention here. *Autoridades* gives two definitions to the term *triaca* (*thriaca*):

(1) Composición de varios simples medicamentos calientes,
en que entran por principal los trocicos de la vívora. Su uso
es contra las mordeduras de animales, e infectos venenosos,
y para restaurar la debilitación por falta del calor natural.
(2) Metaphoricamente vale remedio de algun mal prevenido
con prudencia, o sacado del mismo daño.

Explicit in the second, more figurative definition is the idea that
triacas are paradoxically derived from the very ill that they are
designed to combat. This relates them to that "dangerous"
supplement, the *pharmakon*—both "poison" and "cure"—as
described by Derrida in "Plato's Pharmacy." Writing, as evinced
by Derrida in relation to Plato's *Phaedrus*, appears to have very
much the same ambivalent and self-contradictory force in these
opening scenes of *La cisma*. Inscribed texts, such as the books
and letters that are read and written by the King, can have—
paradoxically—both poisonous and curative effects. The "poison" that is Martin Luther's book may be "cured" by Enrique's.
Written texts can be variously utilized and interpreted and they
always contain—potentially—their own erasures.[9] We shall
shortly see another sense in which writing's supplementarity is
at play in this drama.

The King's role has been, until this point, that of reader and
interpreter of these omens that he has seen in the form of the
dream and in the letters that he has received. But now he attempts to assert more conscious control by injecting himself
into something of a "writerly" role, in terms of reality's omens,
rather than merely being a reader of them. He wants to dictate just
how these particular omens should be read, by placing the letter
from the Pope on his head and the one from Luther at his feet:

> . . . por decir mi grandeza
> cúya la victoria es,
> baje Lutero a mis pies,
> y León suba a mi cabeza.

(157-60)

Alexander A. Parker has noted the metaphorical significance
of this placing of letters by Enrique: " 'Subir a mi cabeza' es
una variante de 'poner sobre la cabeza,' que significa reveren-
ciar; 'bajar a mis pies' se relaciona semánticamente con 'dar

con el pie,' que significa despreciar o repudiar" ("Metáfora" 141). According to Parker, this is just one of a series of images, seen throughout the drama, of "ascent" and "descent." The first of these is related to ambition and pride, the second to *desengaño* and disaster. This same placing of letters occurs, as we have seen, in Lope's *El villano* and in Tirso's *Cautela* with much the same significance: as a ritualistic sign of respect and obedience. Enrique learns very quickly, however, how little writerly control he has even over such symbolic forces, for, opening what he believes is the Pope's letter, he finds—to his great distress—that it is in fact Luther's:

> . . . Mas ¿qué es esto?
> En nuevas dudas me ha puesto
> otro suceso infelice.
> ¡La carta fue de Lutero
> la que sobre mi cabeza
> puse! ¡Qué error! ¡Qué tristeza!
> Otro prodigio, otro agüero
> me amenaza. ¡Muerto soy!
> ¡Santos cielos! ¿Qué ha de ser
> lo que hoy me ha de suceder?
>
> (162-71)

Despite conscious efforts to the contrary, the King is inevitably put into a "readerly" position vis-à-vis these omens. Regardless of the seeming security or finality of a given reading or interpretation, it may always be potentially recontextualized by a further reality, which leaves open the possibility of still further interpretation. Reading is always an implicit act of writing, of active agency, on the part of the reader to render intelligible a given text; it is, therefore, a potentially infinite act, a continuous process that involves not only the primary act of reading, but also re-reading, erasure, and even rewriting.

Once again, however, Volseo diverts Enrique from his desire to read this accidental switching of the letters as an omen of future ills. The Cardinal attempts to reassure the King by telling him that such an occurrence does not fall within the boundaries of what are normally referred to as *agüeros* (173-84) and therefore should not be read as such. Enrique is in fact reassured, but only at the cost of "erasing" and then "rewriting" his initial

interpretation. He therefore rationalizes the Pope's letter's being at his feet by re-interpreting it as his moral "base":

> . . . aqueste error
> ya le juzgo en mi favor,
> y por mi dicha le creo.
> Pues si el Pontífice es
> basa firme y fundamento
> de la fe, como cimiento
> quiso ponerse a los pies.
> Que él es la piedra confieso,
> yo la columna. . . .
>
> (186-94)

We have seen the King's ability to reinterpret or rewrite the
texts with which he is confronted and which he himself has
unconsciously written. He goes on, thus, consciously to erase
and to rewrite his earlier attempt at writing by reversing his
earlier command ("baje Lutero a mis pies / y León suba a mi
cabeza" [159-60]):

> Baje la piedra oprimida,
> suba la llama abrasada,
> ésta en rayos dilatada
> y aquélla del peso herida;
> que yo de las dos presumo
> que buscan en esta acción
> su mismo centro, pues son
> una, piedra, y otra, humo.
>
> (201-08)

The King's use of such imagery as *llamas* and *humo* to describe
Luther's letter emphasizes not only its fiery, "infernal" character, but also its inconstant and variable essence that stands in
stark opposition to the "solid constancy" of the Pope, the "rock"
of Catholic faith ("Peter," from Latin *petra*).

Enrique, however, has been able to impose a reinterpretation
on the accidental switching of these letters only by contradicting
an established cultural precedent: that convention (quoted from
Parker, above) by which placing something on one's head
denotes respect for it and for the person with whom it is
associated, while placing something at one's feet denotes

disrespect. He has inverted the conventional symbolism in order to impose his own private and idiosyncratic system of signification. This erasure and rewriting of cultural precedent
anticipates *La cisma*'s essential action: the implicit erasure of
the very institutions that uphold public order, including the
monarchy itself. But this type of erasure is itself subject to erasure when social order is provisionally re-established in the
drama's final scene.

The opening scenes of *La cisma de Inglaterra* serve very
well, therefore, to characterize Enrique and to anticipate the
tragic events that are to follow. The King is consistently neu-
tralized in his efforts to control or even to make sense out of
the reality that surrounds him. In constantly indulging his need
to re-read, reinterpret, erase, and finally rewrite the texts that
confront him, Enrique helplessly confuses himself before an
ever-shifting, ever-ambiguous reality that is, paradoxically, of
his own creation.

George Mariscal has pointed out that one of the essential
problems of Golden Age Spain was precisely the constitution
of the individual consciousness within a context of psychological and sexual repression: "for seventeenth-century Spanish
culture at large, individual sexuality and interiority must be
subject to the overall social order . . ." (205; cf. Maravall 97).
Enrique's continuing confrontation with various dimensions of
textuality throughout *La cisma* is nothing less than the enactment of the conflict between public and private selves: "the
ideological battle being fought on the field of subjectivity
itself" (Mariscal 200). As private acts, reading and writing constitute the process of self-definition and self-formation. As Paul
Julian Smith tells us, "The magic writing pad is not simply
a metaphor; it points to an originary role for 'writing' (in
Derrida's extended sense) in the constitution of the human
subject" (133).

One important aspect of that "ideological battle" mentioned
above is *La cisma*'s explicitly negative valorization of
Lutheranism relative to Catholicism, precisely in terms of such
self-involved and self-serving impulses. The acts of such
characters as Volseo, Ana, and Enrique—and the results of
those acts—exemplify a selfish individualism that often leads
to disastrous consequences and that, from an orthodox Roman

Catholic point of view, was the earmark of Lutheranism. Indeed, by opposing many aspects of the ecclesiastical hierarchy and thereby breaking the Church's hold on the individual, Lutheranism did help to initiate a general breakdown of authority:

> . . . Luther, by attacking indulgences, was attacking the entire theology and church structure which stood behind them. It was a short step from saying that without contrition the indulgence was invalid to saying that contrition alone, without any papal paraphernalia, was sufficient. Thus, by making salvation dependent on the individual's own faith and contrition, Luther abolished the need for sacraments and a hierarchy to administer them. (Bronowski and Mazlish 83-84)

In opposing such Church institutions as indulgences and the sacraments, Luther was, in effect, attacking many of the observable rituals, the *exterior* forms of the Church. He originally advocated the notion that interior faith was sufficient, that there was no need for prescribed and officially authorized signs of faith such as the sacraments. Interestingly, it is a similar subversion of outer signs, both linguistic and otherwise (and a consequent cynicism about their ability to express accurately an inner reality), that is exemplified and exploited by many of the characters of *La cisma*. But whereas Luther started by advocating the complete abolition of such signs (a position he later abandoned), characters such as Ana and Volseo need them, for it is precisely by undermining both their referential and their institutional value that these characters are enabled to do what they do. From an orthodox Catholic point of view, these characters cause the type of chaos that is the inevitable result of such abusive and self-oriented individualism. The drama thus valorizes Catholicism by positing the need for such "truth-bearing," observable, ceremonial rituals as the sacraments, for they serve as publicly *readable* safeguards against just such abuses.

The relation of Lutheranism to books, in general, also deserves consideration in this context. The King has declared that he is preparing a written defense of the seven sacraments (79-91) in order to combat Luther's thought as expressed in a prior book, the *Captividad Babilonia*. Throughout the beginning of the fifteenth century, a polemical atmosphere was beginning to develop concerning the question of religious faith, the ramifications of which were to have a profound impact for many years to come. Implicit in such a dialectic is a discrepancy—a growing *difference* and perspectivism. The notion had come about that there was room for individual interpretation and personal conscience, as well as the possibility of doing away with, replacing, or even rewriting the "master-text" that the Roman Catholic Church had imposed spiritually and culturally upon the popular sensibility: "For Luther . . . everyone had to decide in his own conscience how the Word of God should be read" (Bronowski and Mazlish 85). Bacigalupo emphasizes the connection between this new relativism and Machiavellian thought:

> The primary implication of Machiavelli's thought was the negation of the medieval social order. . . . with him the hierarchical social system based on the idea that all power emanates from God and on the principle of legitimacy as expressed by Scripture and natural law was destroyed. The State, justice, and law now acquired a quality of moral and theoretical relativity foreign to the Middle Ages. (220)

Mariscal notes the implications of such relativism for seventeenth-century Spain:

> It is particularly difficult for us as post-Enlightenment readers to react to the words "liberty" and "freedom of conscience" as signs of a negative condition, yet within the theological code of Counter-Reformation Spain they signified nothing less than the stepping-off point to social chaos and eternal damnation. (195)

By emphasizing the individual's private sense of faith and by promoting Scripture in the vernacular, Luther opposed the authority of the ecclesiastical hierarchy. It is not by accident that Lutheran doctrine was so intimately related to the relatively new phenomenon of printed books: ". . . Latin and German versions [of Luther's Ninety-Five Theses] were sent to the university press, whence they soon spread throughout Germany. It was, therefore, the new invention—the printing press—which permitted Luther to obtain wide support so quickly and so fully" (Bronowski and Mazlish 82).

150

It is in this sense that the deconstructionist notion of *supplementarity* provides a good model of the way in which Calderón's drama presents Lutheranism, for it is inevitably exhibited as a force of evil. In fact, *La cisma* portrays Lutheranism as a supplement to Roman Catholicism. As such, it is—from a metaphysical point of view—open to all of the usual charges of secondariness, deformation, exteriority, and artificiality. On the other hand, *La cisma* implicitly grants to Roman Catholicism the metaphysical status of a pure transcendent signified, the original meaning and intention of a Divine and Absolute Presence.

This analogy should not be taken too far, however. Derrida uses the concept of supplementarity to discuss, among other things, the ways in which the Western metaphysical tradition has consistently slighted written in favor of oral communication.[10] I would not wish to suggest that Roman Catholicism be identified with a specifically oral modality, of which Lutheranism is a supplemental "writing." By the beginning of the sixteenth century, Catholicism was obviously not orally based. But—again, from an orthodox Roman Catholic point of view—it *did* represent the original Logos, the source of Divine Inspiration. And it is in reference to this absolute and original source, to this Logos, that other faiths were perceived as mere supplements. Such supplements as Lutheranism had to be frowned upon by Catholic orthodoxy, for they represented the potential beginning of an infinite chain of *différance* (both difference and deferral) in relation to the pure and original meaning embodied by Roman Catholic dogma. Such is the essential logocentrism of *La cisma*. This is most ironic, for—again, along Derridean lines—this "pure and original meaning" dictated by Roman Catholic orthodoxy was already, from a Lutheran point of view, infected by *différance*: ". . . what Luther desired at the beginning was a return to primitive Christianity" (Bronowski and Mazlish 89). He considered the Roman Catholicism of his day to be a distortion and bastardization: in short, a *supplement*.

A questioning of the authority and status of books (in the general context of the Reformation and the Counter-Reformation) is foregrounded in *La cisma* by the figure of the King, who is referred to throughout as a *docto*, that is, as a literate and well-read man. The efficacy of the King's formal education is implicitly subverted, however, by the *gracioso* Pasquín, who

is, ironically, the only other character referred to as *docto*.
Shortly after Pasquín makes his first appearance, Catalina
expresses sadness upon seeing his current state, especially in
reference to his past:

> ... me pone triste
> pensar que hombre docto fuiste
> y que con juicio te vi,
> y de verte ahora así
> me pesa, y que estés contento.
>
> (564-68)

His bookish education has not prevented Pasquín from becom-
ing an object of ridicule as court jester.

The idea that formal, book-oriented education has little real
moral influence has been emphasized even earlier in Act I,
when the French ambassador Carlos complains that Volseo has
not permitted him access to the King; Tomás Boleno responds
by referring to the King's formal education:

> No sé yo qué encanto ha sido
> el que Volseo le ha dado
> a un hombre tan celebrado,
> tan prudente y advertido,
> *tan docto y sabio, que bien*
> *leer en escuelas podía*
> *cánones, filosofía,*
> *y teología también.*
>
> (265-72)

Like Pasquín's, the King's formal education has not kept him
from error, for it has done little to protect him from the influence
of such characters as Volseo. Parker notes that "Henry, because
of his passionate nature, is not guaranteed against mistakes by
his intelligence and learning" (*Mind* 260). Books and *filosofía*
have (apparently) little practical moral efficacy where Enrique
is concerned and, in the case of his divorce, even serve to sup-
ply him with the rhetorical means to represent an act that is
rather questionable from an ethical/religious standpoint as a
"defense of the Faith."

When the King does announce his divorce from Catalina, she
appeals to Volseo:

REINA: . . . Cardenal, por Dios, que es solo
                 Juez Supremo, os ruego y pido
                 (ved que en la tierra me pongo)
                 que advirtáis, que aconsejéis
                 bien al Rey.
VOLSEO: El Rey es docto.
                 El se aconseja consigo
                 y con él yo puedo poco.

                                          (2025-31)

Volseo's response is, of course, an out-and-out lie: it was he who had recommended divorce to Enrique in the first place. More importantly, however, it emphasizes a pattern that is consistent throughout: the subversion of conventional signs. Books are the conventional sign of knowledge, which—at least theoretically—leads to wisdom. Enrique does have knowledge in this sense. Ironically, it is precisely such knowledge, acquired by the reading of books, that enables him to commit rather unwise acts. The essentially ambivalent ethical value of books and the knowledge they impart is made explicit by the terms that the *capitán* uses to describe Enrique in *La cisma*'s final verses: ". . . aquí acaba la comedia / del *docto ignorante* Enrique / y muerte de Ana Bolena" (2989-91).

Enrique prefaces and gives authority to his public arguments for the divorce by reiterating his status as a formally educated man:

                     . . . ya sabéis
           que, advertido y cuidadoso
           (bien lo dicen los escritos),
           me llaman Enrique el Docto.

                                          (1821-24)

It is precisely his status as a well-read man that enables him to pull off the divorce without being seriously questioned or challenged by the council of nobles. What is ironic in these words is that the reasoning behind them is circular: the King claims to have authority in this matter because he has studied many books, and this study, he implies, has given him the knowledge and, consequently, the wisdom to make just such royal decisions as this one. But with what authority does he make the claim that he *is* a *docto* in the first place? Naturally, he makes an appeal to the authority of inscription itself: "bien lo dicen los escritos." In these few words, Enrique has implicitly summarized the principal danger of reading and writing: namely, that by virtue of its functionality through absence, all forms of inscription represent a potentially infinite deferral of ultimate meaning and intention. It is precisely this that renders them, in a very real sense, non-referential. Books are powerful because they are self-authorizing: this is what enables them to have both "poisonous" and "curative" effects.

When he considers Volseo's suggestion of divorce, Enrique makes explicit his biblical knowledge by citing scriptural precedent for a man marrying his dead brother's wife (1735-45). But such bookish knowledge does not in the least stop him from publicly using this very argument, soon after, to rationalize his divorce:

> Catalina, nuevo ejemplo
> de virtud (que más dichoso
> que por Rey de dos Imperios
> me tengo por ser su esposo)
> fue de mi hermano mujer:
> esto a todos es notorio;
> y, así, conmigo no pudo
> ser válido el matrimonio.
>
> (1843-50)

By going so consistently against his own purported principles that are based on the study of books such as the Bible, the King's actions in this drama comprise a symbolic negation of those principles and, by extension, of the books that contain them. The King had attempted through his writings to combat Luther's ideology, but his own selfish motivations and acts serve only to exemplify and to confirm, from a Roman Catholic point of view, many of the negative aspects of that ideology. His acts therefore constitute a figurative erasure of his own book, of his own written defense of the Roman Catholic ethic.

Such figurative erasure is—I hope it is now clear—endemic to *La cisma* as a whole, for there is a recurrent subversion and undermining, an insidious erasure, of nearly all written texts, much like that which we have seen earlier and more figuratively in regard to many forms of oral communication. Near the beginning of Act III, for example, Volseo abruptly dismisses several soldiers who have presented some written petitions to

him (2144-49). Not only has Volseo kept such documents from
the King, who, under normal circumstances, would be the one
to receive them: he does not even read them himself. These petitions not only fail to achieve their ultimate goal, that of procuring promotions or appointments for those who have written
them; they also fail as simple acts of communication, for the
message they convey does not reach the consciousness of *any*
recipient, intended or otherwise.

Another example of this undermining of written communication occurs when the King brings Ana a letter—still unopened
and unread—that he has received from Catalina (now living in
exile) and offers it to her (2222-30). In this way, the intended
recipient, Enrique, defers his readerly power to Ana and gives
her full authority over him in regard to it. Ana, however, does
not wish to read it; she tells Enrique that he should indeed read
it and write back to Catalina, that he should respond to her letter with all due pity (2233-41). Enrique is pleased with Ana's
apparent sympathy for Catalina, but this is only another deception; she gives Enrique permission to write back to Catalina,
but only on condition that she may see the letter he writes. Ana
reveals in an aside that her true motive is anything but compas-
sion: "Yo veré / la carta. (Y será porque / en ella ponga veneno)"
(2259-61). Thus, Ana's power over Enrique conditions and
recontextualizes not only his deferred reading of Catalina's letter, but also his written response to it. Enrique's letter in response to Catalina's—ostensibly communicating his pity, but
treated with poison by Ana—will ultimately cause the Queen's
death. Enrique's original intention in writing it, namely, com-
passion, is subverted and transposed into its opposite: cruelty.
This poisoned letter implicitly reiterates Derrida's notion of
pharmakon: writing as poison *and* cure. The letter is comprised
of contrary motifs, for while Enrique's written words will have
a primary curative effect on Catalina's spirit, her very act of
reading them will expose her to the poison that causes her death.

Later in Act III, when the French ambassador Carlos confronts
Ana, accuses her of betraying his love, and rejects her subsequent
rationalizations, he gives back the love letters that she had
written to him: "Toma esos falsos papeles, / toma aquesas
prendas viles" (2620-21). In so doing, he "negates" those
letters: like so many other acts of communication in this drama,
they have been rendered void. Needless to say, Ana's earlier

vows of love to Carlos, both oral and written, have already been
subverted by her own acts of betrayal. Carlos merely acknowledges this symbolically by returning the letters to her.

Unbeknownst to Ana, one of these returned letters has fallen
from her hands. When the King comes out of hiding and finds
it, his worst fears are confirmed, for in it he reads Ana's declaration of love to Carlos. The lost letter thus serves a dual role: it
symbolically erases the love relationship between Carlos and
Ana and serves to negate, in much the same way, Enrique's love
for Ana.

As a result of his discovery of Ana's betrayal, the King disavows his love for her and commands Tomás Boleno, now
presidente of the realm, to imprison her:

> ¡Ay Boleno!
> Tú eres prudente, tú riges
> mi Imperio, tú le gobiernas,
> mi presidente te hice:
> guardarme debes justicia.
>
> (2681-85)

Ironically, it was Ana herself who, by her influence, had put her
father into the office of *presidente* and it is he, therefore, who
must effect her downfall and death by carrying out that office.
The King's written order containing Ana's sentence and execution is perhaps the only efficacious use of writing to be found
in *La cisma de Inglaterra*; that is, it is the only written text in
the drama that is not subverted according to the pattern that is
consistent throughout. This represents an implicit moral valorization of its recipient, Tomás Boleno, who—as we have
seen—is one of the few characters who carries out his public
duty without hesitation. Tomás represents that ethical and civic
presence which is etymologically implied by the name of his
office: *presidente*. This written order is, however (like so many
of the other inscribed texts found in this drama), both deadly
and curative. It is clearly deadly to Ana, but curative and life-
giving insofar as the kingdom at large is concerned.

IV

In Part II of this chapter, I established an essential opposition
between certain characters in relation to those speech acts

called *commissives*. Ana and Volseo consistently go back on their commissives, while others—Catalina, Tomás Boleno, and María—always fulfill theirs. There is one important exception to this rule, on which we should now focus.

In the drama's final scene, the nobles are willing to swear allegiance to María, based upon her promise not to re-establish ties with the Pope. María is unwilling to comply with this condition, but the King convinces both her and the nobility to accept each other, at least provisionally, in the following way:

REY: Efímeras de la edad
           de María son aquéstas.
           Ella es cuerda, y sabrá bien
           moderarse, como cuerda.
           El Reino puede jurarla,
           y si, cuando llegue a Reina,
           no fuere del Reino a gusto,
           depóngala Inglaterra.
           Callad y disimulad,   *A la Infanta.*
           que tiempo vendrá en que pueda
           ese celo ejecutarse,
           ser incendio esa centella.
CAPITÁN: ¿Quiere el Reino hacer la jura?
TODOS: Sí, pues nuestro Rey lo ordena.
TOMÁS: Con las condiciones dichas.
INFANTA: Yo la recibo. *Aparte.* (Sin ellas.)
                 (2968-83; emphasis in original)

There is obvious irony in this final scene, for the King separately promises to each party—the nobility and María—that each will have its way. He thus follows the same strategy that Volseo had earlier used in procuring the support of the French and Spanish kings in his bid for the papacy. As in the case of Volseo and the two foreign kings, the desires of the two parties here are contradictory and cannot both be fulfilled. Furthermore, Enrique sets the stage for further contention and anarchy by saying that, in effect, the oaths given and accepted here today are without value and may be negated in the future, if need be. He tells the nobles that they may dethrone María when she is queen if she does not conform to their wishes in this regard. At the same time, he tells María that she will be able in the future to impose her Faith upon the realm. The empty nature of these ceremonial oaths is made explicit, first of all, by the fact that the nobles pledge their allegiance to María only because the King has ordered them to do so, not because they particularly wish to; and secondly, because María ostensibly accepts the oath, but secretly denies it by rejecting in her aside the conditions that are attached to it.

As we have seen, such duplicity is characteristic of the drama as a whole and infects even the sacred and ceremonial oath of one of its more "ethical" characters, María. This amounts to a theoretical deconstruction of all of those character oppositions established on ethical grounds throughout the entire drama. Given a particular set of circumstances, human failings and limitations are most capable of effecting an erasure of professed codes of morality. María's oath posits a tenuous situation in which good and evil are no longer the terms of an absolute opposition, but are, rather, ambivalently relative and mutually defining. Derrida's description of the ambivalence of the *pharmakon* (quoted in Chapter One) bears repeating here: ". . . it constitutes the medium in which opposites are opposed, the movement and the play that links them among themselves, reverses them or makes one side cross over into the other (soul/body, good/evil, inside/outside, memory/forgetfulness, speech/writing, etc.)" ("Plato's" 127). As a character, María manifests this potential reversibility, and the fact that she does so in the final scene serves to emphasize the drama's overriding sense of moral ambivalence. Like many of the speech acts of *La cisma*, María's oath contains its own potential erasure, its own undoing. As Bacigalupo observes, "In terms of seventeenth-century Spanish political thought Mary's aside 'sin ellas' undoes the absolutely necessary solemnity of such an oath" (224).

The same erasure is at play with regard to the way in which *La cisma* constitutes a figurative rewriting of history as it actually occurred. John Loftis has noted Calderón's deviation from history, as opposed to Shakespeare's relative fidelity to it in *Henry VIII*:

> Despite the historical materials with which he worked, Calderón did not write a history play but a *comedia*. . . . Shakespeare, on the other hand, wrote an English history or chronicle play in which fidelity to recorded history, though not essential in details, guides the structural pattern. Shakespeare achieved the truth of history, Calderón the truth

of poetry—at least for those of his readers or spectators who accept his Roman Catholic assumptions. ("Henry VIII" 222)

The Catholicism that María intends in her zeal to impose on England in the drama's final scene will ultimately be negated by the forces of the Reformation. Calderón's fictional version of English history is therefore part of a chain of *différance*—reading, writing, interpretation, erasure, and rewriting—that is potentially limitless and that is itself represented metaphorically in the very action of the play.

The entire drama is framed by two acts of communication that reflect one another in their own subversion of the very codes that enable their existence. At the beginning of *La cisma*, in the context of his dream, the King's writings are erased by an unknown woman, who, in effect, cancels them, turns them into an anticommunication. María's final oath of office is subverted (or implicitly deconstructed) in much the same way by her own aside, for her oath contains its own figurative erasure. It is from precisely such erasure that *La cisma de Inglaterra* derives its tragic force. Calderón's drama represents a chaotic world of darkness: a world in which communication, both oral and written, is self-deconstructing, self-erasing; a world in which communicative signifiers are either totally unfaithful to the signifieds that they ostensibly represent or are rendered powerless by the circumstances in which they are produced. Given the logocentric nature of Calderón's ideological stance, his literary portrait of King Henry VIII's Protestant England could have none other than the deviant, secondary, and subversive status of the supplement.

Supplement

If one may judge by the evidence offered in Chapter Three, in which Mira de Amescua's *El ejemplo mayor de la desdicha* is examined, and in Chapter Four, which deals with Tirso's *Cautela contra cautela,* there remains little doubt that written and inscribed texts have tremendous structural and thematic importance in many of the *dramas de privanza.* In an unpublished doctoral dissertation (1957), Sister Mary Austin Cauvin observes that inscribed documents often appear in these dramas and although she does not deal with them in any kind of detail or depth, she feels that they are important enough to be included in her final chapter as one of the defining characteristics of the genre. She notes that among various motifs imported from the *comedia de capa y espada* into these dramas are love letters that may complicate the intrigue without any tragic result. But she also observes that:

> in the *comedia de privanza* love letters may . . . be instrumental in causing disaster to the *privado* where they are misconstrued by his sovereign. Or the incriminating letters may be forged documents of a serious political nature which brand the *privado* as a traitor. Or this type of letter may be *bona fide* but of such a nature that it is capable of being understood as treachery on the part of the writer who was acting in good faith. (472-73)

Cauvin's brief characterization of these documents makes plain their functional importance in the *dramas de privanza*, a judgment which will be verified by a brief perusal of a number of them.

Mira de Amescua's *La próspera fortuna de Bernardo de Cabrera* and its sequel, *La adversa fortuna . . .* (1634)[1] are likewise dominated by written documents, as are two dramas considered to be prototypes for all of the *dramas de privanza*, Damián Salucio del Poyo's diptych *La próspera* and *La adversa fortuna de Ruy López de Avalos* (1612?). It could be argued that the frequent appearance of inscription as a motif in these dramas is simply a matter of influence: that since the dramas that served as models for all of the others contained many written texts, the works they inspired do, as well. Another possibility is that the written word is simply a natural part of the intrigue of courtly existence. It is a common critical observation that an important aspect of these dramas is the mutability of human fate. We have seen in Mira de Amescua's *El ejemplo* that the unknowability of fate is one dimension of the larger question of the limitations of human understanding and the consequent ambiguity of human experience: a problem of epistemology. The potential ambiguity and secrecy of the written word are an appropriate part of the atmosphere of secrecy and courtly intrigue that these dramas enact. As such, written texts are the literalization—the worldly manifestation—of a more symbolic writing, the unknowable text of Fate. Written texts, therefore, are undoubtedly an integral part of the *dramas de privanza* and could reasonably be considered one of their generic characteristics.

Other genres of Golden Age drama also utilize written texts in an interesting way. Certain *comedias de santo*—which typically represent martyrdoms, some historical, some not—begin with the protagonist reading a scriptural, historical, or philosophical text that provides the thematic core around which much of the drama's action will revolve, the philosophical or moral truth of which the plot is a literalization or enactment. At the beginning of Calderón's *El mágico prodigioso* (1637), for example, Cipriano, a pagan philosopher, is attempting to understand and interpret a passage from Pliny's *Natural History* which gives the following definition of the "true" God: "Dios es una bondad suma, / una esencia, una sustancia, / todo vista, todo manos" (610a). Driven by passion for Justina (who is a Christian), Cipriano attempts to seduce her. When she rejects him, he offers his soul to the Devil in exchange for her seduction. The Devil is, however, unable to tempt Justina away from her resolute faith and deliver her to him, as they had agreed. Cipriano thereby realizes that the Devil's magic is false and he experiences a conversion that leads him to know the God that he had only read about at the beginning of the drama: one who is all-knowing, all-powerful, and all-good. This type of intertextuality, whereby a passage from an authoritative text provides the thematic key to the drama's action, is also found in such dramas as *Los dos amantes del cielo* (1636?) and *El gran príncipe de Fez* (1668?), both by Calderón. Each of these *comedias* enacts a metaphysics of presence by way of orality, whereby an inscribed text must be "proven" by subjecting it to the test of "living" dialogic reality.

Inscription is also functional in Calderón's honor plays. In *El médico de su honra* (1629?), Mencía's guilt is ostensibly proven to her jealous husband Gutierre by way of a series of misunderstandings that culminates when he discovers her writing (in all innocence) a note to Enrique, the man of whom he is suspicious. After Gutierre has unjustly had his wife bled to death, it is a form of figurative inscription—the blood stain left secretly on the door to Gutierre's house by the surgeon whom he had forced to perform the bleeding—that leads the King to discover the crime. When Gutierre is absolved of all guilt for his cruel treatment of Mencía, we are left with the uneasy feeling that his crime has been "erased" in the name of a cultural inscription that has guided all of his actions: the honor code itself.

Another of Calderón's honor plays, *El pintor de su deshonra* (1648?), utilizes the motif of painting—yet another form of inscription—as a manifestation of the honor code. In effect, Don Juan Roca is the painter (the originator or "writer") of his own dishonor, which is nothing other than a self-projection based upon a cruel and outmoded code of social behavior; much like *El médico de su honra*, *El pintor* is a rather explicit criticism of the socially inscribed economy of male honor in which "Women . . . serve as objects of exchange, both excluded from and essential to the male circulation whose operation they precede" (Paul Julian Smith 164).

A word must be said here about writing and the question of history. Each of the dramas discussed in these essays has some basis in actual history, but necessarily constitutes a rewriting of it. *El villano*'s basis is perhaps less tangible than the others', for it portrays no specifically factual event. Moreover, by the final scene (which, as many critics have noted, contains many of the ritual elements of an *auto sacramental*), Juan Labrador and the King have taken on a symbolic quality that is reminiscent of allegory. Nevertheless, its depiction of the process of social inclusion by way of the institution of the monarchy is historically and culturally valid, if not factually specific. Lope's drama is, in effect, an adherence to the neo-Aristotelian conception of poetic truth as being preferable to the truth of contingent historical fact(s).

The same may be said of the other dramas as well. Their aim is obviously not history, but rather an "erasure" and rewriting of history from a contemporary viewpoint and in accordance with contemporary culture, aesthetics, and ideology, all themselves forms of *inscription*. *La estrella de Sevilla*'s portrayal of King Sancho is an extrapolation based upon the popular myth surrounding the historical King Sancho since the time of his reign. It is, in effect, a poetic justification of his title "el Bravo," a justification that was inspired in part by contemporary preoccupations about the nature, limitations, and public responsibilities of the monarchy. Mira de Amescua's *El ejemplo*, like many of the *dramas de privanza*, responded to contemporary public concerns about the status of the court favorite. The story of Belisario was well known, and Mira rewrites some of the historical characters in the interest of dramatic art, that is, in order to express a poetic truth, not facts. Tirso's *Cautela contra cautela* likewise examines the institutional status of the *privado*, but also constitutes a fascinating and self-reflexive examination of courtly intrigue that was itself a form of theatricalization. Calderón's *La cisma de Inglaterra* represents perhaps the most radical rewriting of history as it actually occurred: Princess María did not come immediately to power, as portrayed in the final scene, nor does her attempted imposition of Roman Catholicism ever take hold in England, although it is certainly arguable that the eventuality of factual history—the continuation of the schism—is implied by the conditions surrounding the drama's close.[2]

Each of the dramas examined in this study represents writing and inscription in a different way. *El villano* enacts the institutional power of the written word by contrasting Juan Labrador's inscribed epitaph with the letters by which the King ultimately includes him within the sphere of civic life. The written word functions in Lope's play as a force of socialization. In this sense, *La estrella de Sevilla* constitutes an inversion of *El villano*, for King Sancho effects social subversion and dishonor precisely through the use of written documents, but is finally forced to live up to civic and institutional responsibility by way of the opposite form of communication: the spoken word. *El ejemplo* utilizes written texts and inscription as the literalization of a more figurative and inscrutable text: the mutability and ambiguity of human experience and fate. *Cautela* utilizes the same ambivalence, based upon *papeles* and metatheater, that is found in *El ejemplo*, but exploits that ambivalence to an even greater degree in order to examine one of the fundamental epistemological concerns of the entire Golden Age: fiction versus truth, appearance versus reality. Finally, *La cisma* utilizes various dimensions of textuality—reading, re-reading, writing, rewriting, and erasure—as the privileged space of self-definition: the place where ideologies do battle and where language (potentially) undoes itself.

Spain's Golden Age is a time of transition and crisis that encompasses many radical changes in sensibility, in knowledge, and in the very concept of reality. It is a period of profound questioning and doubt as to the status of the newly widespread institution of written and printed texts. Consequently, it is clear that the ideological basis of these dramas lies squarely within the metaphysics of presence (the tradition of logocentrism), for each of them portrays the written word as a potentially evil and subversive force. The only exception to this rule is the first drama studied, *El villano en su rincón*, in which the written word is utilized by the King to re-establish the social order that is symbolically undermined by Juan Labrador. But even in Lope's play, the written word as a force of social order is ultimately subordinated to orality, for Juan must come to live at court, in the full presence of the King, in order to be integrated fully into society. In effect, writing is used in *El villano* as a merely supplementary means to an ideal and transcendent end: the presence of orality.

The questions opened up by writing and inscription offer many possible areas of future investigation. I have touched on only a few in this brief Supplement. I believe that one of the most fertile of these will prove to be the *dramas de privanza*, on which very little work has been done in any regard. But the other subgenres mentioned (the *comedias de santo* and the honor plays) also offer rich possibilities in the way of figurative forms of inscription. Writing and inscription surely offer a wealth of concepts and strategies by which the culture of Spain's Golden Age—as part of the beginning of "modernity"—may be explored.

Notes

Introduction

1. See Bibliography for editions of dramas used. Verse numbers are indicated in parentheses immediately following quotations, except for those editions (such as the Aguilar edition of Tirso's *Cautela contra cautela*) which do not offer a verse count, in which case page number and column letter are indicated. All emphasis within quotations is mine, except where otherwise indicated.

2. I am especially grateful to Professor Daniel L. Heiple of Tulane University for bringing both this sonnet and Professor Silverman's essay to my attention.

3. Robert Alter's *Partial Magic: The Novel as a Self-Conscious Genre* (1975) brilliantly traces the novelistic tradition of self-referentiality that begins with Cervantes.

4. The obvious exception to this rule is the communication made possible by such modern technology as telephone, radio, and television. Such technology, however, preserves the oral/aural dimension of the spoken communicative act and therefore retains the dialogical spontaneity of actual presence.

5. Two other contemporary theorists who have noted and discussed the connection between writing and death are Michel Foucault (*Language* 116-17) and, from a very different point of view, Jacques Derrida ("Plato's" 91-92).

6. Ong's thinking here constitutes an unmistakable echo of Augustine's *Confessions* (XI.27): "Let us consider the sound of a bodily voice. The voice begins to sound, it sounds, it continues to sound, and then it stops sounding. Now there is silence; the voice is past and is no longer a voice. Before it began to sound, it was in the future and could not be measured because it did not yet exist, and now it cannot be measured because it no longer exists. Therefore, it could only be measured while it was actually sounding, because only then was there something in existence which could be measured. But even then it was not static; it was going, and going away into the past . . ." (279).

7. The linguist Edward Sapir uses the term *drift* to describe the process by which dialects are formed: "Language moves down time in a current of its own making. It has a drift. If there were no breaking up of a language into dialects, if each language continued as a firm, self-contained unity, it would still be constantly moving away from any assignable norm, developing new features unceasingly and gradually transforming itself into a language so different from its starting point as to be in effect a new language" (150). Derrida, on the other hand, uses the term to refer specifically to one of the defining characteristics of the production and reception of written texts. It is clear, however, that the two uses are related by their common emphasis on the process by which *différance* (meaning both "difference" and "deferral") comes into play.

8. The Spanish term *ley* derives from Latin *lex*, which is etymologically related to both *legis* ("word") and *legere* ("to read"), thus the intimate connection between the law and the written word.

9. *Theatro de los theatros de los passados y presentes siglos* (1689-90).

Chapter One
Cultural Inscriptions: The Written and the Spoken in Lope's *El villano en su rincón*

1. Other critics who have taken particular note of the paradoxical nature of Juan's epitaph are Casalduero (48) and Wardropper ("La venganza" 768-69).

2. I have here borrowed terminology utilized by Searle ("Taxonomy" 1-29).

3. Fray Miguel Agustín's *Libro de los secretos de agricultura, casa de campo, y pastoril*, originally written in Catalán (1617) and translated by the author to Castilian (1625), contains several warnings about the potential dangers of all written texts, in a section concerning the proper upbringing of young women in rural areas:

> Tintero, pluma, ni papel en su poder no lo han de tener, ni escrivirán cosa alguna, sino fuere en presencia del señor, ó señora, consultandoles aquello que havrán escrito, por vér si está bien, y con buen termino, ahora sean letras missivas, oraciones, devociones, ó qualquier otra cosa.
>
> Si algun hombre, ó muger las llevase alguna carta, ó villete, dirigidos á ellas, aunque la persona que la lleve sea conocida, y de confianza, y aunque supiesse quien la ha escrito, y fuesse la persona mas conjunta, y de segura confianza, no la tomarán de ninguna manera, antes les respondrán la dén á su señor, ó señora ó de ninguna manera la tomen de manos de otros, ni la lean que primero no tengan licencia del señor, ó la señora, y leida primero por alguno de ellos. (28)

I am very grateful to Professor Thomas Capuano of Northeast Missouri State University for bringing this passage to my attention.

4. For a more detailed consideration of these songs, see Rodríguez, "Los cantables."

5. Like Juan had done earlier for the King's benefit (in the case of the lamb with the knife tied around its neck), the King at this point explains his own use of symbols to Juan: the scepter is the "insignia" of his power and reign, the mirror represents the monarchy as a function of social self-awareness and unity (that is, as a form of "mirror" in which the kingdom is to observe and unify itself), and the sword symbolizes the justice which he dispenses as king.

6. For further discussion of Juan Labrador's relation to death, see Casalduero (53) and Wardlaw (114).

Chapter Two
Presence and Absence in *La estrella de Sevilla*

1. Controversy over this drama's paternity has continued most recently with the work of Alfredo Rodríguez López-Vázquez, who, following the lead of Sturgis E. Leavitt in *The "Estrella de Sevilla" and Claramonte* (1931), has made the case for Andrés de Claramonte as its author.

2. The bibliography on honor in Golden Age drama is immense. One of the clearest explanations of the concept is still Gustavo Correa's "El doble aspecto de la honra en el teatro del siglo XVII" (1958).

3. This idea may be found throughout Derrida's writings, but is perhaps most prevalent in *Of Grammatology* (see especially ch. 2, "Linguistics and Grammatology").

4. Aside from its first definition of *bronce*, ". . . metal compuesto de la mezcla de cobre y estaño," the *Diccionario de Autoridades* (subsequently referred to as *Autoridades*) gives a second, more figurative one: ". . . por analogía vale firmeza, perpetuidad, y cosa durable."

5. 1422-26; 2116-17; 2774-77. Clarindo, the play's *gracioso*, makes the final reference to bronze, which ends the drama:

> . . . esta tragedia os consagra
> Cardenio, dando a *La Estrella*
> *de Sevilla* eterna fama,
> *cuyo prodigioso caso*
> *inmortales bronces guardan.*
>
> (3025-29)

The drama turns back upon itself in this final moment and, in a gesture of self-reference, takes the immortalizing capacity of bronze and applies it to all the action of *La estrella de Sevilla*. In these words, the drama becomes the "bronze" that will preserve these events for future memory.

6. Ruth L. Kennedy observes Busto's preference for honor that is born of one's own acts ("*La Estrella*" 391) as well as the significant frequency with which the term *justo* is contrasted with *gusto* (388-89).

7. *The King's Two Bodies: A Study in Medieval Political Theology* (13). See William C. McCrary's fine application of Kantorowicz's thesis to *La estrella* (506). Kantorowicz's thesis is, of course, eminently applicable to a wide range of *comedias*.

8. Sancho himself had unknowingly anticipated his own action during his prior discussion with the King:

> . . . a voces, señor, os pido,
> *aunque él mi hermano sea,*

> o sea deudo, o amigo
> que en el corazón se emplea,
> el riguroso castigo
> que tu autoridad desea.
>   Si es así, *muerte daré*,
> *señor, a mi mismo hermano*,
> y en nada repararé.

(1516-24)

Chapter Three
"Seeing and Not Seeing": Interpretation and Drift in Mira de Amescua's *El ejemplo mayor de la desdicha*

1. The "wonderful" in Butcher's translation.

2. Such literalization on the level of action is, of course, very characteristic of much Golden Age drama (Wardropper, "Dramatization").

Chapter Four
Dangerous Scripts in Tirso's *Cautela contra cautela*

1. I have found only a single article that is specifically devoted to it: Ruth Lee Kennedy's "Tirso's *Cautela contra cautela*: Its Authenticity in His Theatre and Its Importance." As indicated by its title, Professor Kennedy's article establishes thematic relations between *Cautela* and other dramas by Tirso, but is by no means a thorough analysis of the drama itself.

2. Page numbers and column are indicated in parentheses.

3. Elena's purely material orientation is further emphasized when Porcia later asks her for money to give to the man she loves. Elena cynically assumes that Porcia needs the money in order to buy the man's affections: "¡Porcia ha de amar obligando! / Sangre de un Rey procedida, / ¿ha de comprar ser querida?" (935b).

4. Blanco Aguinaga et al.: ". . . el abismo, en suma, entre el ser y el parecer así como la obsesión por el engaño y desengaño, son la clave de una lectura significativa del Barroco" (289).

5. Cf. Sullivan 101-13. Sullivan's text is perhaps the clearest and best articulated analysis of Tirso's dramatic technique, an important aspect of which is his consistent use of metatheater.

6. In Lope's *El villano en su rincón*, we remember, Juan Labrador likewise places a letter from the King upon his head, as a sign of respect.

7. Sullivan: ". . . there exists a conspiratorial triangle between author, protagonist, and audience. The manipulator is carrying out Tirso's dramatic will in an illusory situation and is endowed with special intellectual gifts and privileges to allow the realization of a specific goal. At the same time, the manipulator has all the data to which we the audience have access. This conspiratorial privilege continues since the manipulator largely determines the play's action" (112).

8. Sullivan devotes an entire chapter to the multivalent quality of Tirso's language: ". . . his success in forcing multiplicity of effect into single words and phrases. This practice I have termed a prismatic use of language, since a single term may fragment into a plurality of connotations or meanings within its context" (149).

9. Porcia's advice to Alfonso is noteworthy in its similarity to that passage from *El ejemplo mayor de la desdicha* in which Belisario attempts to convince the Emperor that he is innocent despite all appearances to the contrary (see Chapter Three, above):

> Entre las cosas más claras
> ojos engañados vimos;
> los remos parecen corbos
> en las ondas y zafiros
> del mar, y paloma negra
> suele volar, y, a los visos
> del sol, parecer sus alas
> oro y púrpura de Tiro.
> Pues si en el agua y el sol
> vemos engaños, rey mío,
> ¡en las lenguas de los hombres
> cuantas veces se habrán visto!
>
> (2526-37)

10. Sullivan ch. 1, "The Cultural and Intellectual Background of Spain in the Counter Reformation."

Chapter Five
Calderón's *La cisma de Inglaterra* and the Ethics of Erasure

1. Bacigalupo thus characterizes the essential isolation of the principal characters: "Henry, Wolsey, and Ann constantly and unwittingly isolate themselves from the source of legitimate political authority, namely, divine and natural law. Their isolation is not fortuitous since their policies and deceits create a state of confusion and irrationality in which the fundamental limitations of the possibilities open to men are no longer acknowledged" (216).

2. In the introduction to his edition of *La cisma*, Ruiz Ramón observes the stylistic contrast between Carlos's long and rhetorical praise of Ana's beauty (in *octavas reales*) and the much shorter and more direct way (in *octosílabos*) in which he expresses misgivings about her character (17-18).

3. Nicholas Shumway observes that many distinct elements of the Reformation were blurred by Calderón, at least insofar as it is portrayed in the *autos*. Thus many aspects of the Reformation, such as Protestantism, Lutheranism, and Calvinism, were often subsumed by the single term *Lutheranism*.

4. See Alexander A. Parker's discussion of this parable (*Mind* 267).

5. Ruiz Ramón observes in his edition that Pasquín is engaging in wordplay with *bella* and *bellaca* (99n616). *Autoridades*'s third definition of *bellaco* is interesting in this respect: "Lo propio que malo, perverso, y ajeno de razón: y así se dice Acción bellaca, pensamiento bellaco." Such wordplay implicitly reiterates the radical discrepancy, noted above, between Ana's exterior physical beauty and her "uglier" interior motives.

6. The following discussion is based upon John R. Searle's *Speech Acts* (1974).

7. Ruiz Ramón identifies this type of confusion as one of the characteristic elements of Calderón's special sense of the "tragic" (Introduction 41-42).

8. Cf. Erich Auerbach, "Figura," for a detailed discussion of this term.

9. Derrida often places words *sous rature* ("under erasure") by writing the word, crossing it out, and then including both word and deletion. The concept of erasure serves to emphasize the impossibility of representing a full, absolute, and final meaning; it is a manifestation of the inexorable play of *différance* in language.

10. Although the example of Plato's *Phaedrus* has been pointed out as part of this tradition, it must be said at the same time that Plato's attitude toward orality versus writing is not nearly so clear-cut as might be thought. Eric A. Havelock, in *Preface to Plato*, makes it clear that *The Republic* constitutes a sustained attack on the *episteme* that is molded and handed down by the oral epic tradition. (See, in particular, chs. 2, 8, 9, 10.)

Supplement

1. Until recently, both were ascribed to Lope; MacCurdy (83) attributes them to Mira de Amescua.

2. Parker explains the historical background of *La cisma* and justifies Calderón's radical rewriting of factual history in terms of cultural and religious sensibility, as well as the tendency toward poetic and dramatic unity (*Mind* 280-87).

Bibliography

Abel, Lionel. *Metatheatre: A New View of Dramatic Form*. New York: Hill, 1963.

Agustín, Fray Miguel. *Libro de los secretos de agricultura, casa de campo, y pastoril*. 1617. Tarragona: Catedral, 1980.

Alter, Robert. *Partial Magic: The Novel as a Self-conscious Genre*. 1975. Berkeley: U of California P, 1978.

Andrews, J. R., S. G. Armstead, and J. H. Silverman. "Two Notes for Lope de Vega's *El viliano en su rincón*." *Bulletin of the Comediantes* 8 (1966): 33-35.

Aníbal, C. E. "Observations on *La Estrella de Sevilla*." *Hispanic Review* 2 (1934): 1-38.

Aristotle. *Poetics*. Trans. S. H. Butcher. New York: Hill, 1961.

Arrondíz, Othon. *La influencia italiana en el Renacimiento de la comedia española*. Madrid: Gredos, 1969.

Atkins, G. Douglas. *Reading Deconstruction, Deconstructive Reading*. Lexington: UP of Kentucky, 1983.

Auerbach, Erich. "Figura." Trans. Ralph Manheim. *Neue Dantestudien*. Istanbul, 1944. Rpt. in *Scenes from the Drama of European Literature*. Minneapolis: U of Minnesota P, 1984. 11-76.

Augustine. *The Confessions*. Trans. Rex Warner. New York: Mentor-Omega, 1963.

Austin, J. L. *How to Do Things with Words*. Cambridge: Harvard UP, 1978.

Azar, Inés. "*La Estrella de Sevilla*, or How to Speak Up like a King." Unpublished essay, 1988.

Bacigalupo, Mario Ford. "Calderón's *La cisma de Ingalaterra* and Spanish Seventeenth-Century Political Thought." *Symposium* 28 (1974): 212-27.

Bances Candamo, Francisco. *Theatro de los theatros de los passados y presentes siglos*. 1689-90. Ed. Duncan Moir. London: Tamesis, 1970.

Bandera, Cesáreo. *Mimesis conflictiva: ficción literaria y violencia en Cervantes y Calderón*. Madrid: Gredos, 1975.

Barthes, Roland. *Image, Music, Text*. Trans. Stephen Heath. New York: Hill, 1977.

——. *Mythologies*. Trans. Annette Lavers. New York: Hill, 1972.

——. *Writing Degree Zero*. Trans. Annette Lavers and Colin Smith. New York: Hill, 1968.

173

Bataillon, Marcel. "El villano en su rincón." *Varia lección de clásicos españoles*. Madrid: Gredos, 1964. 329-72.

Belsey, Catherine. *Critical Practice*. New York: Methuen, 1980.

Bentley, Eric. "The Universality of the *Comedia*." *Hispanic Review* 38 (1970): 147-62.

Benveniste, Emile. *Problème de linguistique générale*. Paris: Gallimard, 1966.

Birkhead, Henry. "The Schism of England: Calderón's Play and Shakespeare's." *Modern Language* 10 (1928): 36-44.

Blanco Aguinaga, Carlos, Julio Rodríguez Puértolas, and Iris M. Zavala. *Historia social de la literatura española*. Madrid: Castalia, 1978.

Bloom, Harold, et al. *Deconstruction and Criticism*. 1979. New York: Continuum, 1986.

Borges, Jorge Luis. *Ficciones*. 1956. Madrid: Alianza, 1982.

Bradbury, Gail. "Irregular Sexuality in the Spanish *Comedia*." *Modern Language Review* 76.3 (1981): 566-80.

Brancaforte, Benito. "Lope's *El villano en su rincón*: A Vision of Universal Harmony." Ebersole 49-66.

Bronowski, Jacob, and Bruce Mazlish. *The Western Intellectual Tradition: From Leonardo to Hegel*. 1960. New York: Harper, 1962.

Brooks, J. L. "*La Estrella de Sevilla*: 'Admirable y famosa tragedia.'" *Bulletin of Hispanic Studies* 32 (1955): 8-20.

Brown, Sandra L. "Goodness and *El villano en su rincón*." *Romance Notes* 14 (1972): 551-56.

Burke, James F. "The *Estrella de Sevilla* and the Tradition of Saturnine Melancholy." *Bulletin of Hispanic Studies* 51 (1974): 137-56.

Burke, Peter. *Popular Culture in Early Modern Europe*. New York: New York UP, 1978.

Cabantous, Max. "Le Schisme d'Angleterre vu par Calderón." *Les Langues Neo-Latines* 62 (1968): 43-58.

Cabrera, Vicente. "*La Estrella de Sevilla*: Prosodic Evidence of Interpolations in the Text." *Language Quarterly* 12 (1972): 11-14.

Calderón de la Barca, Pedro. *La cisma de Inglaterra*. Ed. Francisco Ruiz Ramón. Madrid: Castalia, 1981.

——. *El mágico prodigioso. Obras completas*. Vol. 1. Ed. A. Valbuena Briones. Madrid: Aguilar, 1969.

Calvino, Italo. *If on a Winter's Night a Traveler*. 1979. Trans. William Weaver. New York: Harcourt, 1981.

Camp, Jean. "Cómo Lope de Vega imaginaba a Francia: visión de Francia en Lope y especialmente en *El villano en su rincón.*" *Cuadernos Hispanoamericanos* 161-62 (1963): 421-26.

Casalduero, Joaquín. "Sentido y forma de *El villano en su rincón.*" *Estudios sobre el teatro español.* Madrid: Gredos, 1967. 547-64.

Cauvin, Sister Mary Austin. "The 'comedia de privanza' in the Seventeenth Century." Diss. U of Pennsylvania, 1957.

Cervantes Saavedra, Miguel de. *El ingenioso hidalgo don Quijote de la Mancha.* Ed. Luis Andrés Murillo. Madrid: Castalia, 1978.

Cohen, Walter. *Drama of a Nation: Public Theatre in Renaissance England and Spain.* Ithaca: Cornell UP, 1985.

Correa, Gustavo. "El concepto de la fama en el teatro de Cervantes." *Hispanic Review* 27 (1959): 280-302.

——. "El doble aspecto de la honra en el teatro del siglo XVII." *Hispanic Review* 26 (1958): 99-107.

——. "El doble aspecto de la honra en *Peribáñez y el Comendador de Ocaña.*" *Hispanic Review* 26 (1958): 188-99.

Correa Calderón, Evaristo, and Fernando Lázaro. *Lope de Vega y su época.* Salamanca: Anaya, 1961.

Corriere, Alex. "Pierre Lebrun's Adaptation of *La Estrella de Sevilla.*" *Xavier University Studies* 3 (1964): 11-18.

Cruickshank, D. W. "Literature and the Book Trade in Golden Age Spain." *Modern Language Review* 73 (1978): 799-824.

Culler, Jonathan. *On Deconstruction.* Ithaca: Cornell UP, 1982.

——. *The Pursuit of Signs: Semiotics, Literature, Deconstruction.* Ithaca: Cornell UP, 1981.

——. *Structuralist Poetics: Structuralism, Linguistics and the Study of Literature.* 1975. Ithaca: Cornell UP, 1982.

Curtius, Ernst Robert. *European Literature and the Latin Middle Ages.* 1948. Trans. Willard R. Trask. New York: Harper, 1963.

Darst, David H. "Teorías de la comedia en el siglo de oro de España." *Boletín de la Biblioteca Menéndez Pelayo* 62 (1986): 17-36.

Davies, R. Trevor. *The Golden Age of Spain (1501-1621).* New York: Harper, 1961.

Dawson, S. W. *Drama and the Dramatic.* 1970. London: Methuen, 1984.

de Armas, Frederick A. "The Apples of Colchis: Key to an Interpretation of *La Estrella de Sevilla.*" *Forum for Modern Language Studies* 15 (1979): 1-13.

175

de Armas, Frederick A. "Balthasar's Doom: Letters that Heal/Kill in Claramonte's *El secreto en la mujer*." (Forthcoming).

———. "The Hunter and the Twins: Astrological Imagery in *La Estrella de Sevilla*." *Bulletin of the Comediantes* 32 (1980): 11-32.

Derrida, Jacques. *Of Grammatology*. 1967. Trans. Gayatri Chakravorty Spivak. Baltimore: Johns Hopkins UP, 1976.

———. "Plato's Pharmacy." *Dissemination*. 1972. Trans. Barbara Johnson. Chicago: U of Chicago P, 1981.

———. *Positions (Interviews)*. 1972. Trans. Alan Bass. Chicago: U of Chicago P, 1981.

———. "Signature Event Context." *Limited Inc*. Trans. Samuel Weber and Jeffrey Melman. Evanston, IL: Northwestern UP, 1988.

———. *Writing and Difference*. Trans. Alan Bass. Chicago: U of Chicago P, 1978.

Diccionario de Autoridades. Real Academia Española. 1726. Edición facsímile. Madrid: Gredos, 1984.

Dixon, Victor. " 'Beatus nemo': *El villano en su rincón*, las 'Poliantas' y la literatura de emblemas." *Cuadernos de Filología* 3 (1981): 279-300.

Dulsey, Bernard. "*La Estrella de Sevilla*, ¿Adónde va?" *Hispanófila* 2 (1958): 8-10.

Dunn, Peter N. "Honour and the Christian Background in Calderón." *Bulletin of Hispanic Studies* 37 (1960): 75-105.

———. "Irony as Structure in the Drama." *Bulletin of Hispanic Studies* 61 (1984): 317-25.

———. "Patrimonio del alma." *Bulletin of Hispanic Studies* 41 (1964): 78-85.

Eagleton, Terry. *Literary Theory: An Introduction*. Minneapolis: U of Minnesota P, 1983.

Ebersole, Alva V., ed. *Perspectivas de la comedia*. Colección Siglo de Oro, Estudios de *Hispanófila* 6. Valencia: Artes Gráficas Soler, 1978.

Elam, Keir. *The Semiotics of Theatre and Drama*. London: Methuen, 1980.

Elias, Norbert. *The Court Society*. 1969. Trans. Edmund Jephcott. New York: Pantheon, 1983.

Encyclopedia of Philosophy. Ed. Paul Edwards. 2nd ed. New York: Macmillan, 1972.

Entrambasaguas, Joaquín de. *Lope de Vega y su tiempo: estudio especial de "El villano en su rincón."* Barcelona: Teide, 1962.

La estrella de Sevilla. Diez comedias del Siglo de Oro. Ed. Hymen Alpern and José Martel. 2nd ed. New York: Harper, 1968.

Fiore, Robert L. *Drama and Ethos: Natural Law Ethics in Spanish Golden Age Theater.* Lexington: UP of Kentucky, 1975.

Fischer, Susan L. "Reader-Response Criticism and the 'Comedia': Creation of Meaning in Calderón's *La cisma de Ingalaterra.*" *Bulletin of the Comediantes* 31 (1979): 109-25.

Fish, Stanley. "How to Do Things with Austin and Searle: Speech-Act Theory and Literary Criticism." *Is There a Text in This Class? The Authority of Interpretive Communities.* Cambridge: Harvard UP, 1980. 197-245.

Flew, Anthony. *A Dictionary of Philosophy.* 2nd ed. New York: St. Martin's, 1984.

Foucault, Michel. *The Order of Things: An Archaeology of the Human Sciences.* Trans. anon. New York: Vintage, 1973.

——. *Language, Counter-memory, Practice: Selected Essays and Interviews.* Trans. Donald F. Bouchard and Sherry Simon. 2nd ed. Ithaca: Cornell UP, 1980.

Fox, Dian. "The 'Villano' in His Corner: Supercorrection of the Pseudo-humanist." *Refiguring the Hero: From Peasant to Noble in Lope de Vega and Calderón.* University Park: Penn State UP, 1991. 58-76.

Frye, Northrup. *Anatomy of Criticism: Four Essays.* 1957. Princeton: Princeton UP, 1973.

Gerstinger, Heinz. *Pedro Calderón de la Barca.* Trans. Diana Stone Peters. New York: Ungar, 1973.

González-Marcos, Máximo. "El anti-absolutismo de *La Estrella de Sevilla.*" *Hispanófila* 74 (1982): 1-24.

Goody, Jack. *The Logic of Writing and the Organization of Society.* Cambridge: Cambridge UP, 1986.

Gutiérrez, Jesús. *La "fortuna bifrons" en la comedia hasta 1630.* Santander: Sociedad Menéndez Pelayo, 1975.

Halkhoree, Premraj. "Lope de Vega's *El villano en su rincón*: An Emblematic Play." *Romance Notes* 14 (1972): 141-45.

Hamilton, T. Earle. "Spoken Letters in the 'Comedias' of Alarcón, Tirso, and Lope." *PMLA* 62 (1947): 62-75.

Harland, Richard. *Superstructuralism: The Philosophy of Structuralism and Post-Structuralism.* London: Methuen, 1987.

Havelock, Eric A. *Preface to Plato.* New York: Grosset, 1967.

Hawkes, Terence. *Structuralism and Semiotics*. Berkeley: U of California P, 1977.

Herbold, Anthony. "Shakespeare, Calderón, and Henry VIII." *East-West Review* 2 (1965): 17-32.

Hesse, Everett W. "The Sense of Lope's *El villano en su rincón.*" *Essays on Spanish Letters of the Golden Age*. Madrid: Studia Humanitatis, 1981. 68-83.

——. "The Sociology of Lope's *El villano en su rincón.*" *The Comedia and Points of View*. Potomac, MD: Scripta Humanistica, 1984. 34-45.

Highet, Gilbert. *The Classical Tradition: Greek and Roman Influences on Western Literature*. 1949. Oxford: Oxford UP, 1976.

Holman, C. Hugh. *A Handbook to Literature*. 4th ed. Indianapolis: Bobbs-Merrill, 1980.

Holy Bible (Revised Standard Version). Cleveland: Meridian, 1962.

Ife, B. W. *Reading and Fiction in Golden Age Spain*. Cambridge: Cambridge UP, 1985.

Jakobson, Roman. "Closing Statement: Linguistics and Poetics." *Style in Language*. Ed. Thomas A. Sebeok. Cambridge: MIT P, 1966. 350-77.

Johnson, Elmer D. *Communication: An Introduction to the History of Printing, Books, and Libraries*. Metuchen, NJ: Scarecrow, 1973.

Jones, C. A. "Honor in Spanish Golden Age Drama: Its Relation to Real Life and Morals." *Bulletin of Hispanic Studies* 35 (1958): 199-210.

——. "Tragedy in the Spanish Golden Age." *The Drama of the Renaissance: Essays for Leicester Bradner*. Ed. Elmer M. Blistein. Providence: Brown UP, 1970. 100-07.

Jones, R. O. "Poets and Peasants." Kossoff and Amor y Vázquez 341-55.

——, ed. *Studies in Spanish Literature of the Golden Age, Presented to Edward M. Wilson*. London: Tamesis, 1973.

Jung, C. G. *The Practice of Psychotherapy: Essays on the Psychology of the Transference and Other Subjects. The Collected Works*. Vol. 16. Trans. R. F. C. Hull. New York: Pantheon, 1954.

Kantorowicz, Ernst. *The King's Two Bodies: A Study in Medieval Political Theology*. Princeton: Princeton UP, 1957.

Kennedy, Ruth L. "*La Estrella de Sevilla*, Reinterpreted." *Revista de Archivos, Bibliotecas y Museos* 78 (1975): 385-408.

Kennedy, Ruth L. "Tirso's *Cautela contra cautela*: Its Authenticity in His Theatre and Its Importance." *Revista de Archivos, Bibliotecas y Museos* 75 (1968-72): 325-53.

Kermode, Frank. *The Genesis of Secrecy: On the Interpretation of Narrative*. Cambridge: Harvard UP, 1979.

Kossoff, A. David, and José Amor y Vázquez, eds. *Homenaje a William L. Fichter: estudios sobre el teatro antiguo hispánico y otros ensayos*. Madrid: Castalia, 1971.

Küpper, Joachim. *"La cisma de Inglaterra* y la concepción calderoniana de la historia." *Hacia Calderón*. Ed. Hans Flasche. Stuttgart: Franz Steiner, 1988. 183-201.

Larson, Catherine. *Language and the Comedia*. Lewisburg: Bucknell UP, 1991.

Lauer, A. Robert. "The Pathos of Mencía's Death in Calderón's *El médico de su honra*." *Bulletin of the Comediantes* 40.1 (1988): 25-40.

Lauria, Donatella. *La poetica di Calderón de la Barca ne "La cisma de Inglaterra."* Catania: Bonanno, 1976.

Leavitt, Sturgis E. "Apples of Hesperides in the *Estrella de Sevilla*." *Modern Language Notes* 45 (1930): 314.

———. *The "Estrella de Sevilla" and Claramonte*. Cambridge: Harvard UP, 1931.

———. *Golden Age Drama in Spain: General Considerations and Unusual Features*. Chapel Hill: U of North Carolina P, 1972.

———. *An Introduction to Golden Age Drama in Spain*. Madrid: Castalia, 1971.

Lewis, Charlton. *A Latin Dictionary*. 3rd ed. London: Oxford UP, 1980.

Lipmann, Stephen. "Metatheater and the Criticism of the *Comedia*." *Modern Language Notes* 91 (1976): 231-46.

Loftis, John. "Henry VIII and Calderón's *La cisma de Ingalaterra*." *Comparative Literature* 34.3 (1982): 208-22.

———. *Renaissance Drama in England and Spain*. Princeton: Princeton UP, 1987.

Loud, Mary. "Pride and Prejudice: Some Thoughts on Lope de Vega's *El villano en su rincón*." *Hispania* 58.4 (1975): 843-50.

MacCurdy, Raymond R. *The Tragic Fall: Don Alvaro de Luna and Other Favorites in Spanish Golden Age Drama*. Chapel Hill: U of North Carolina Dept. of Romance Languages, 1978.

Maravall, José Antonio. *Teatro y literatura en la sociedad barroca*. Madrid: Seminarios y Ediciones, 1972.

Mariana, Juan de. *Historia general de España*. Madrid: Sánchez, 1650.

Mariscal, George. "Calderón and Shakespeare: The Subject of Henry VIII." *Bulletin of the Comediantes* 39.2 (1987): 189-213.

Martínez, Christine D. "Alejandro y Diógenes: inversión e ironía en *El villano en su rincón* de Lope de Vega." *Bulletin of the Comediantes* 43.1 (1991): 21-30.

Martins, Hector. "*La Estrella de Sevilla* como emblema." *Barroco* 1 (1969): 75-79.

McCrary, William C. "Ritual Form and Action in *La Estrella de Sevilla*." Kossoff and Amor y Vázquez 505-13.

McLuhan, Marshall. *The Gutenberg Galaxy: The Making of Typographic Man*. Toronto: Toronto UP, 1962.

Merchant, Moelwyn. *Comedy*. London: Methuen, 1985.

Mira de Amescua, Antonio. *El ejemplo mayor de la desdicha. Teatro* Vol. 2. Ed. Angel Valbuena Prat. Clásicos Castellanos. Madrid: Espasa-Calpe, 1928.

Moir, Duncan W. "Lope de Vega's *Fuenteovejuna* and the *Emblemas morales* of Sebastián de Covarrubias Horozco (with a few remarks on *El villano en su rincón*)." Kossoff and Amor y Vázquez 537-46.

Molina, Tirso de. *Cautela contra cautela. Obras dramáticas completas*. Vol. 2. Ed. Blanca de los Ríos. Madrid: Aguilar, 1946.

Muecke, D. C. *Irony and the Ironic*. London: Methuen, 1982.

Newels, Margaret. *Los géneros dramáticos en las poéticas del Siglo de Oro*. London: Tamesis, 1974.

Norris, Christopher. *Deconstruction: Theory and Practice*. London: Methuen, 1982.

——. *Derrida*. Cambridge: Harvard UP, 1987.

Nowell, Charles E. *A History of Portugal*. 1952. Princeton: Van Nostrand, 1962.

O'Connor, Thomas A. "Is the Spanish *Comedia* a Metatheater?" *Hispanic Review* 43 (1975): 275-89.

——. "Metatheater and the *Comedia*: A Further Comment." *Modern Language Notes* 92 (1977): 336-38.

Olson, Elder. *Teoría de la comedia. (The Theory of Comedy.)* Trans. Bruce W. Wardropper. Barcelona: Ariel, 1978.

Ong, Walter J. *Interfaces of the Word*. Ithaca: Cornell UP, 1977.

——. *Orality and Literacy: The Technologizing of the Word*. New York: Methuen, 1982.

——. *The Presence of the Word*. New York: Simon, 1970.

Paredes, Alejandro L. "Nuevamente la cuestión del metateatro: *La cisma de Ingalaterra*." *Actas del Congreso Internacional sobre Calderón y el teatro español del siglo de oro*. Madrid: Consejo Superior de Investigaciones Científicas, 1983.

Parker, Alexander A. "Henry VIII in Shakespeare and Calderón: An Appreciation of *La cisma de Ingalaterra*." *Modern Language Review* 43 (1948): 326-52.

———. "Metáfora y simbolismo en la interpretación de Calderón." *Actas del Primer Congreso Internacional de Hispanistas*. Ed. Frank Pierce and Cyril A. Jones. Oxford: Dolphin, 1964. 141-60.

———. *The Mind and Art of Calderón: Essays on the "Comedias."* Cambridge: Cambridge UP, 1988.

———. "The Spanish Drama of the Golden Age: A Method of Analysis and Interpretation." *The Great Playwrights*. Vol. 1. Ed. Eric Bentley. New York: Doubleday, 1970. 679-707.

———. "Towards a Definition of Calderonian Tragedy." *Bulletin of Hispanic Studies* 39 (1962): 222-37.

Parr, James A. "An Essay on Critical Method, Applied to the *Comedia*." *Hispania* 57 (1974): 434-44.

Plato. *"Phaedrus" and Letters VII & VIII*. Trans. Walter Hamilton. London: Penguin, 1983.

———. *The Republic*. Trans. Francis MacDonald Cornford. New York: Oxford UP, 1945.

Pratt, Mary Louise. *Toward a Speech Act Theory of Literary Discourse*. Bloomington: Indiana UP, 1977.

Preminger, Alex, ed. *Princeton Encyclopedia of Poetry and Poetics*. Princeton: Princeton UP, 1965.

Preminger, Alex, Leon Golden, O. B. Hardison, Jr., and Kevin Kerrane, eds. *Classical Literary Criticism: Translations and Interpretations*. New York: Ungar, 1974.

Price, R. M. "A Note on Fortune in *El villano en su rincón*." *Journal of Hispanic Philology* 6.1 (1981): 66-72.

Recoules, Henri. "Cartas y papeles en el teatro del siglo de oro." *Boletín de la Real Academia Española* 54 (1974): 479-96.

Reichenberger, Arnold G. "The Uniqueness of the *Comedia*." *Hispanic Review* 27 (1959): 303-16.

Ricoeur, Paul. *Interpretation Theory: Discourse and the Surplus of Meaning*. Fort Worth: Texas Christian UP, 1976.

Rivers, Elias L. "Plato's *Republic* and Cervantes' *Don Quixote*: Two Critiques of the Oral Tradition." *Studies in Honor of Gustavo Correa*. Potomac, MD: Scripta Humanistica, 1986. 170-76.

Bibliography

Rivers, Elias L. *Quixotic Scriptures*. Bloomington: Indiana UP, 1983.

——. "The Shame of Writing in *La Estrella de Sevilla*." *Folio* 12 (1980): 105-17.

——. "Written Poetry and Oral Speech Acts in Calderón's Plays." *Aureum Saeculum Hispanum: Beiträge zu Texten des Siglo de Oro*. Ed. Karl-Hermann Korner and Dietrich Briesermeister. Wiesbaden: Steiner, 1983. 271-84.

Rodríguez, Alfredo. "Los cantables de *El villano en su rincón*." Kossoff and Amor y Vázquez 639-45.

Rodríguez López-Vázquez, Alfredo. "*La Estrella de Sevilla* y Claramonte." *Criticón* 21 (1983): 5-31.

——. "*La Estrella de Sevilla* y *Deste agua no beberé*: ¿un mismo autor?" *Bulletin of the Comediantes* 36 (1984): 83-110.

Ruggiero, Michael J. "Dramatic Conventions and Their Relationship to Structure in the Spanish Golden Age *Comedia*." *Revista Hispánica Moderna* 37 (1972-73): 137-54.

——. "Some Approaches to Structure in the Spanish Golden Age *Comedia*." *Orbis Litterarum* 28 (1977): 173-91.

——. "The Term *Comedia* in Spanish Dramaturgy." *Romanische Forschungen* 84 (1972): 277-96.

Ruiz Ramón, Francisco. "Funciones dramáticas del hado en *La cisma de Inglaterra*." *Approaches to the Theater of Calderón*. Ed. Michael D. McGaha. Washington: UP of America, 1982. 119-28.

——. *Historia del teatro español desde sus orígenes hasta 1900*. Madrid: Alianza, 1971.

——. Introduction. *La cisma de Inglaterra*. By Pedro Calderón de la Barca. Ed. Ruiz Ramón. Madrid: Castalia, 1981. 7-58.

Salomon, Nöel. *Recherches sur le thème paysan dans la "comedia" au temps de Lope de Vega*. Bordeaux: Institut d'Etudes Ibériques et Ibéro-Américaines de l'Université de Bordeaux, 1965.

Sánchez Escribano, Federico, and Alberto Porqueras Mayo. *Preceptiva dramática española del Renacimiento y el Barroco*. Madrid: Gredos, 1965.

Sapir, Edward. *Language: An Introduction to the Study of Speech*. 1921. New York: Harcourt, 1949.

Saussure, Ferdinand de. *Course in General Linguistics*. Trans. Wade Baskin. New York: McGraw, 1966.

Searle, John R. *Speech Acts: An Essay in the Philosophy of Language*. London: Cambridge UP, 1974.

Searle, John R. "A Taxonomy of Illocutionary Acts." *Expression and Meaning*. Cambridge: Cambridge UP, 1979.

——. "What Is a Speech Act?" *Language and Social Context: Selected Readings*. 1972. Ed. Pier Paolo Giglioli. London: Penguin, 1975. 136-54.

Shivers, George R. "La unidad dramática de *La cisma de Inglaterra*." Ebersole 133-43.

Shumway, Nicholas. "Calderón and the Protestant Reformation: A View from the *Autos sacramentales*." *Hispanic Review* 49.3 (1981): 329-48.

Silverman, Joseph H. "Personaje y tipo literario: el converso." *El personaje dramático: ponencias y debates de las VII jornadas de teatro clásico español* (Almagro, 20 al 23 de septiembre, 1983). Madrid: Taurus, 1985. 253-61.

Smith, Barbara Herrnstein. *On the Margins of Discourse: The Relation of Literature to Language*. 2nd ed. Chicago: U of Chicago P, 1983.

Smith, Paul Julian. *Writing in the Margin: Spanish Literature of the Golden Age*. Oxford: Oxford UP, 1988.

Sturm, Sara H., and Harlan G. Sturm. "The Astronomical Metaphor in *La Estrella de Sevilla*." *Hispania* 52 (1969): 193-97.

——. "The Two Sancho's in *La Estrella de Sevilla*." *Romanistisches Jahrbuch* 21 (1970): 285-93.

Sullivan, Henry W. *Tirso de Molina and the Drama of the Counter Reformation*. Amsterdam: Rodopi, 1976.

Toro, Alfonso de. "Aproximaciones semiótico-estructurales para una definición de los términos *tragedia*, *comedia*, y *tragicomedia*: el drama de honor y su sistema." *Gestos* 1 (1986): 53-72.

Varey, John E. "Towards an Interpretation of Lope de Vega's *El villano en su rincón*." Jones, R. O., *Studies* 315-37.

Vega, Lope de. *El galán escarmentado*. *Obras*. Vol. 1. Madrid: Real Academia, 1916.

——. "*El villano en su rincón*" y "*Las bizarrías de Belisa*." Ed. Alonso Zamora Vicente. Madrid: Espasa-Calpe, 1963.

Wade, Gerald E. "Elements of a Philosophical Basis for the Interpretation of Spain's Golden Age Comedy." *Studia Ibérica: Festschrift für Hans Flasche*. Ed. Karl-Hermann and Klaus Rühl Korner. Bern: Francke, 1973. 589-602.

——. "Spain's Golden Age Culture and the 'Comedia.'" *Hispania* 61 (1978): 832-50.

Wardlaw, Frances Day. *"El villano en su rincón*: Lope's Rejection of the Pastoral Dream." *Bulletin of Hispanic Studies* 58 (1981): 113-19.

Wardropper, Bruce W. "La comèdia española del Siglo de Oro." Olson 181-242.

——. "The Dramatization of Figurative Language in the Spanish Theatre." *Yale French Studies* 47 (1972): 189-98.

——. "La imaginación en el metateatro calderoniano." *In honorem R. Lapesa*. Madrid: Gredos, 1974. 613-29.

——. "The Implicit Craft of the Spanish 'Comedia.'" Jones, R. O., *Studies* 339-56.

——. "La venganza de Maquiavelo: *El villano en su rincón*." Kossoff and Amor y Vázquez 765-72.

——, ed. *Siglos de Oro: Barroco. Historia y crítica de la literatura española*. Vol. 3. Barcelona: Crítica, 1980.

Weiner, Jack. "Zeus y la metamorfosis de Sancho IV en *La Estrella de Sevilla*." *Explicación de Textos Literarios* 10.1 (1981): 63-67.

Wellek, Rene, and Austin Warren. *Theory of Literature*. 1942. New York: Harcourt, 1956.

Wilson, E. M., and Duncan Moir. *Siglo de Oro: Teatro. Historia de la literatura española*. Vol. 3. Ed. R. O. Jones. Barcelona: Ariel, 1982.

Wilson, Margaret. *Spanish Drama of the Golden Age*. London: Pergamon, 1969.

Zamora Vicente, Alonso. "Estudio preliminar." *"El villano en su rincón" y "Las bizarrías de Belisa*." By Lope de Vega. Madrid: Espasa-Calpe, 1963. vii-cxxiii.

Ziomek, Henryk. *A History of Spanish Golden Age Drama*. Lexington: UP of Kentucky, 1984.

Index

Absence. *See* Presence vs. absence
Admiratio, 67-68
Agustín, Fray Miguel, 168n3. *See also* City vs. country
Alter, Robert, 16, 167n3
Ambivalence, 83-87, 105-08, 111-13. *See also* Appearance vs. reality
Appearance vs. reality, 70-72, 91-96, 101-05, 109-14, 120-24, 133, 165, 170n4, 171nn9 and 2, 172n5. *See also* Ambivalence
Aristotle, 67, 164. *See also* Admiratio
Augustine, Saint, 167n6. *See also* Ong, Walter J.
Austin, J. L., 58. *See also* Speech act theory
Azar, Inés, 50

Bacigalupo, Mario, 150, 158, 171n1
Bances Candamo, Francisco, 18, 168n9
Barthes, Roland, 5-6. *See also* Writing
Bataillon, Marcel, 24-25
Beatus ille, 30, 31, 36. *See also* City vs. country
Blanco Aguinaga, Carlos, et al., 170n4. *See also* Appearance vs. reality
Books, 16, 139-40, 145, 149-54 history of, 10-12, 16
Borges, Jorge Luis, 2-3
Bronowski, Jacob, and Bruce Mazlish, 150, 151. *See also* Lutheranism
Brooks, J. L., 44-46, 54. *See also* Honor

Calderón de la Barca, Pedro
   La cisma de Inglaterra, 18,

114, 115-59, 164, 165, 171n2, 172n2
   writing
      desk, 115-16, 138
      "dream," 139-44
      Enrique's book, 140, 149-50
      erudition, 151-54
      letters from Luther and Pope León X, 145-49
      love letters, 155-56
      poisoned letter, 155
   Los dos amantes del cielo, 163
   El gran príncipe de Fez, 163
   El mágico prodigioso, 162-63
   El médico de su honra, 163
   El pintor de su deshonra, 163
   La vida es sueño, 130
Calvino, Italo, 2-3
Capa y espada, comedia de, 18-19, 161
Carnival, 112-14
Casalduero, Joaquín, 168n1, 169n6
Catholicism. *See* Roman Catholicism
Cauvin, Sister Mary Austin, 161. *See also* Privanza, drama de
Chiasmus, 38-39, 158. *See also* Derrida, Jacques; Pharmakon
City vs. country, 26-27, 29-32, 34-39, 168n3. *See also* Agustín, Fray Miguel; *Beatus ille*
Claramonte, Andrés de, 14, 169n1
Correa, Gustavo, 43, 169n2. *See also* Honor
Counter-Reformation. *See* Reformation/Counter-Reformation
Country. *See* City vs. country
Culture. *See* Nature vs. culture
Curtius, Ernst Robert, 11-12. *See also* Books

de Armas, Frederick A., 14
Death. *See* Writing: and death
Derrida, Jacques, 6-10, 15, 75-76,
142, 145, 155, 167n7, 169n3,
172n9. *See also* Chiasmus;
Différance; Drift; Inscription;
Pharmakon; Supplement; Writing
and honor code, 46
"magic writing pad," 141, 148
and Ong, Walter J., 9-10
"Plato's Pharmacy," 8-9, 39, 158
Determinism, 130-31, 133, 140.
See also Lutheranism; Prophecy
Différance, 9, 63, 151, 159, 172n9.
See also Derrida, Jacques
defined, 167n7
Disjunction, 47, 70, 90
Divorce, 134-35
Dixon, Victor, 25
Drift, 6-7, 9, 75-76, 79-82, 102.
See also Derrida, Jacques; Writing
defined, 167n7

Elam, Keir, 14
Epitaph, 17, 22-26, 28, 34-35,
37-38
Erasure, 9, 18, 135, 138-41, 144-48,
154-59, 165. *See also* Derrida,
Jacques; Writing
defined, 172n9
Estrella de Sevilla, La, 17, 41-63,
91, 103, 123, 164-65, 169nn5-8
authorship of, 41, 169n1
writing
death sentence, 59-61, 63
Estrella's letter, 57-58, 62
inscription in bronze, 47-48,
169n5
marriage contract, 50-51, 62
petitions, 48-49, 62
royal decrees, 50-51, 55, 62
Exteriority. *See* Interiority vs.
exteriority

Fate, 17, 65, 72, 87-90, 133-34,
137, 162, 165

Fish, Stanley, 134. *See also*
Speech act theory
Foucault, Michel, 167n5. *See also*
Writing
Free will, 117, 129-31, 133-34, 140
Freud, Sigmund, 141

Golden Age, 2, 10, 12-16, 19, 36,
88, 104-05, 162, 165-66
Gracioso, 131-33, 143-44,
151-52

Hamilton, T. Earle, 12-13. *See
also* Writing in the *comedia,*
criticism of
Havelock, Eric A., 172n10. *See
also* Plato; Writing
Honor, 2, 16, 122-23, 138-39,
163, 169n2
and Derrida, Jacques, 46
honra vs. *honor,* 43-46, 48-49,
53-54, 58-59, 63
and morality, 43-46
and obligation, 47
and presence, 42-43, 46, 52
Honor play, 163, 166
Honra. See Honor: *honra* vs.
honor

Identity (self), 63, 120, 148-49,
165. *See also* Unconscious
Ife, B. W., 10-11. *See also* Books
Individualism, 148-49
Inscription, 7-8, 14-15, 29, 31-34,
38-39, 40, 73, 163-64. *See also*
Derrida, Jacques; Writing
Interiority vs. exteriority, 97, 117,
120-24, 133, 142, 149, 172n5.
See also Appearance vs. reality

Jung, C. G., 141

Kantorowicz, Ernst, 51, 169n7
Kennedy, Ruth L., 169n6, 170n1
Kermode, Frank, 113. *See also*
Spirit vs. material

"King's Two Bodies, The," 51,
169n7. *See also* Public vs. private

Larson, Catherine, 14, 91
Letters, 1-2, 12-13, 17, 27-29,
32-34, 73, 75-77, 79-82, 90,
103-04, 144-48, 155, 164-65.
See also Love letters
placed on head, 28, 105, 145-48,
170n6
Loftis, John, 158-59
Logocentrism, 7, 102, 151, 159,
165. *See also* Derrida, Jacques;
Metaphysics of presence
Loud, Mary, 27-28
Love, 94, 96-99. *See also* Love
letters
Love letters, 1, 155-56, 161
Luther, Martin, 127, 140, 144-51.
See also Lutheranism
Lutheranism, 127, 131, 133-34,
140, 144-51, 171n3. *See also*
Books; Protestantism; Reforma-
tion/Counter-Reformation;
Supplement

MacCurdy, Raymond R., 65, 67,
87-88, 172n1. *See also* Pri-
vanza, drama de
Machiavelli, Niccolò, 150
"Magic writing pad," 141, 148.
See also Derrida, Jacques;
Unconscious
Maravall, José Antonio, 32-33
Mariscal, George, 148, 150
Material. *See* Spirit vs. material
McCrary, William C., 52, 61,
169n7
Memory, 8-9, 39, 47-48, 158
*Menosprecio de corte, alabanza
de aldea,* 36. *See also* City vs.
country
Metaphysics of presence, 6-9,
46, 60-61, 102, 109, 114, 163,
165. *See also* Derrida, Jacques;
Logocentrism

Metatheater, 18, 143, 164-65,
170n5. *See also* Papel; Rivers,
Elias L.; Role-playing
Mira de Amescua, Antonio
*El ejemplo mayor de la des-
dicha,* 17, 65-90, 91, 94,
100, 102, 104, 106, 108,
123, 161, 162, 164, 165,
171n9
writing
inscribed coins, 74
inscribed rings, 72-74
*Comedia de Píramo y
Tisbe,* 83-87
letters, 75-77, 79-81
order of punishment,
81-82
petitions, 77-78
La próspera and *La adversa
fortuna de don Bernardo de
Cabrera,* 161
Modernity, 20, 39-40, 166
Molina, Tirso de [*pseud. of*
Gabriel Téllez]
Cautela contra cautela, 18,
91-114, 123, 146, 161, 164,
165, 170n1
writing
anonymous warning,
102-04, 114
French king's signature,
110-12
King's letter, 105
King's orders, 112-13
petitions, 102
Porcia's letter, 99-102

Nature vs. culture, 38-40. *See
also* City vs. country
Negotium. See Otium/negotium

Ong, Walter J., 3-5, 7. *See also*
Metaphysics of presence;
Writing
and Augustine, Saint, 167n6
and Derrida, Jacques, 9-10

Oral tradition. *See* Writing: and oral tradition
Otium/negotium, 35-37

Palimpsest, 141. *See also* Identity (self); Unconscious; Writing
Papel, 1-2, 15, 17, 55-56, 83-87, 104-05, 107, 110, 112, 114, 165. *See also* Metatheater; Rivers, Elias L.; Role-playing
Parker, Alexander A., 44, 92, 145-46, 147, 152, 172n2
Passion. *See* Reason vs. passion
Pharmakon, 9, 14, 39, 145, 154-58. *See also* Chiasmus; Derrida, Jacques; Supplement; Writing
defined, 8
Plato. *See also* Logocentrism; Metaphysics of presence
Phaedrus, 8-9, 39, 141-42, 145, 158, 172n10
The Republic, 172n10
Play within the play, 83-87, 104-08, 110, 112. *See also* Metatheater
Poetic justice, 44, 82-83
Presence vs. absence, 3-7, 9, 12, 30-34, 39-40, 42-43, 46, 51-54, 56-57, 60-63, 76, 80-81, 106-07, 115-20, 134
Printing press, 10-12, 16. *See also* Books
Privado. *See* Privanza, drama de
Privanza, drama de, 17, 65, 87, 104-05, 161-62, 165-66. *See also* MacCurdy, Raymond R.
Private. *See* Public vs. private
Prophecy, 131-34, 137
Protestantism, 18, 117, 119-20, 159, 171n3. *See also* Lutheranism; Reformation/Counter-Reformation
and determinism, 131-33
Public vs. private, 32-37, 51-55, 60, 117-20, 124-28, 131-32, 140-41, 148, 156, 164

Reading, 2-3, 10-11, 21, 57, 80-81, 91, 117-18, 139, 142-43, 159, 165
Reality. *See* Appearance vs. reality
Reason vs. passion, 117, 128, 139, 141. *See also* Unconscious
Recoules, Henri, 13. *See also* Writing in the *comedia*, criticism of
Reformation/Counter-Reformation, 114, 151, 159, 171nn3 and 10. *See also* Lutheranism; Protestantism
Reichenberger, Arnold G., 117
Right vs. left, 141-43
Rivers, Elias L., 13-14, 16, 41, 42-43, 47, 50, 56, 63, 83, 104. *See also* Honor; Metatheater; *Papel;* Role-playing
Role-playing, 83-87, 104-05, 108-09, 113, 114, 124. *See also* Metatheater; *Papel;* Rivers, Elias L.
Roman Catholicism, 10, 18, 114, 117, 127-28, 131, 133, 140, 148-51, 158-59, 164
Ruiz Ramón, Francisco, 129, 132, 133-34, 171n2, 172nn5 and 7

Salucio del Poyo, Damián. *See also* Privanza, drama de
La próspera and *La adversa fortuna de Ruy López de Avalos*, 162
Santo, comedia de, 162-63, 166
Sapir, Edward, 167n7. *See also* Drift
Searle, John R., 135, 168n2, 172n6. *See also* Speech act theory
Shumway, Nicholas, 171n3. *See also* Lutheranism; Protestantism; Reformation/Counter-Reformation
Signifier/signified, 44, 96-99, 101-02, 105, 109, 113-14
Silverman, Joseph H., 1-2

Smith, Barbara Herrnstein, 5
Smith, Paul Julian, 14, 15, 38, 39, 148, 163
Soliloquy, 31-32
Sonnet, 1-2, 29-31
Speaking. *See* Writing: vs. speaking
Speech act theory, 24, 46, 134-38, 156-57. *See also* Fish, Stanley; Searle, John R.
Spirit vs. material, 97, 99, 101, 113-14, 170n3. *See also* Appearance vs. reality; Interiority vs. exteriority; Signifier/signified
Sturm, Harlan, and Sara Sturm, 55
Subversion, linguistic, 91, 119
Sullivan, Henry W., 170nn5 and 7, 171nn8 and 10
Supplement, 9, 15, 46, 111, 113, 114, 151, 159, 165. *See also* Derrida, Jacques; Logocentrism; Pharmakon; Writing
    defined, 7
Symbol, 34-35, 38, 74, 125, 138, 168n5

Téllez, Gabriel. *See* Molina, Tirso de

Unconscious, 115-18, 138-39, 141, 147. *See also* Identity (self); "Magic writing pad"; Reason vs. passion; Writing
Unity of action, 92

Varey, John E., 23
Vega, Lope de
    Fuenteovejuna, 14
    El galán escarmentado, 1-2
    Peribáñez, 38-39
    El villano en su rincón, 16-17, 21-40, 46, 53, 74, 103, 118, 139, 146, 163, 164, 165, 170n6
        writing
            epitaph, 17, 22-26, 28, 34-35, 37-38
            erudition, 29-31

Lisarda and writing, 26-27
King's letters, 27-29, 32-33
King's decree, 38
Visual imagery, 66, 111-12. *See also* Ambivalence; Appearance vs. reality; Fate
    admiración, 67-68
    darkness (blindness), 70, 72, 90, 93-94, 131
    seeing, 65, 68-70

Wardlaw, Frances Day, 25, 169n6
Wardropper, Bruce W., 18-19, 32, 168n1
Wilson, Margaret, 43. *See also* Honor
Writing. *See also* Books; Derrida, Jacques; *Différance;* Drift; Inscription; Letters; Ong, Walter J.; Pharmakon; Supplement
    contracts, 50-51
    and death, 3-4, 22-23, 35, 167n5
    and history, 23-24, 48, 163-64, 172n2
    and monumentality, 5-6, 24-25
    and oral tradition, 29-31, 168n4, 172n10
    vs. speaking, 3-6, 15-16, 26-27, 38-39, 56-57, 61-63, 90, 100-02, 106, 142, 151, 165
Writing in the *comedia,* criticism of, 12-14